Tactical Influence:

How I Countered

an Insurgency with Words

By Mitchell C. Hockenbury

This book is dedicated to you. Though it contains my story, once you implement its lessons, it becomes yours. I'm honored you are here.

Introduction: The Day We Lost Five

Later, soldiers told news reporters that they'd seen the streets go strangely quiet. People suddenly disappeared, and a millisecond before it happened, they knew something was wrong. But earlier that morning, the day of January 28, 2008, we had no idea what was coming.

We'd been in Mosul, Iraq, for three weeks, and it was our platoon's first day off. Things had been tough since we'd arrived. We'd responded to attacks on other units, been shot at with small arms fire, and taken hits from improvised explosive devices. At night, we'd conducted raids, always without enough sleep. The previous night's raid ended at 4 a.m., and the men were having a well-earned break.

As Platoon Leader, I was up and working in the command post, a small modular office from where we ran operations. My second-in-command and good buddy, Sergeant First Class Rick Chewning, sat next to me. Chewy, as we called him, was teasing me over yet another disastrous Miami Dolphins season. I was just happy they'd won one game and wouldn't go down as the worst football team in history. We were debating their prospects for next year when a breathless soldier burst into the command post.

"Get your platoon ready to go. Now!" he said. Chewy and I looked at each other, and I knew he was thinking the same as me. *This can't be good*. As Chewy gathered the men, I received our orders. Another platoon had run into trouble while out on a mission, and one of their Humvees was disabled. We were to escort the recovery vehicle that would tow it back to base. I wondered why the breathless soldier was so intense about a simple vehicle recovery, but I didn't have time to dwell on it. We were heading outside the wire.

Outside the Wire

That day was dreary and overcast. It had recently rained, turning anything dirt into thick, sticky mud. The streets had huge potholes—bomb craters, actually—that filled with water and became muddy pits. As we drove around a corner, I saw our target ahead. It wasn't just a disabled Humvee; it was a completely destroyed carcass of a vehicle. It sat in a fresh crater the width of the entire road. An improvised explosive device must have detonated directly beneath it. *How did anyone survive that blast?* I thought.

We dropped off a squad at a nearby house to watch over the rest of us from an elevated position. Then we headed towards the crater, where I set up two Bradley Fighting Vehicles on each side the disabled vehicle. Being the size of small tanks, the Bradleys would help us secure the area so the recovery vehicle could hook up to the disabled Humvee and tow it away.

The battalion commander called through on the radio and asked if one of our squads could assist with the recovery.

"Affirmative," I said. I jumped out of the Bradley, ready to help hook up the destroyed Humvee when the battalion commander waved me over. *What's our most senior officer doing here, in person?* I thought.

The battalion commander spoke quietly.

"Mitch, we can't find everyone," he said. "Can your guys help?" *Can't find everyone?* The words rattled me. I looked over to the large field alongside the road and saw two soldiers carrying a body bag. It finally sunk in: The men *hadn't* survived the blast. We weren't just recovering a vehicle.

"Roger, Sir," I said, and instructed a team to search the field with me.

It was muddy and my boots sunk between clumps of overgrown grass and weeds. Amidst piles of filthy, discarded trash, I made out the camouflage pattern of combat uniform. I'd found one of ours. I hollered and another guy ran up with a body bag. He grabbed the fallen soldier under the arms, and I lifted the legs—well, what was left of them.

The sight of the torn limbs wrecked me, but I tried to focus and be gentle. We began to zip the body bag shut, and it dawned on me that I would never see this man again. I wanted to know his name. I held back the zipper and leaned forward to read his name tape, but it was caked in mud. Not a single letter was visible. Then the soldier assisting me zipped up the bag. The moment was gone. I'd never know who he was.

There was more of him—and others—to be found, and we weren't about to leave any part of them behind. The search continued. Someone discovered a far-flung boot with a foot inside. I found a radio and other pieces of blown-apart equipment. They were what we call *sensitive items*—things the enemy could use to intercept our communications. Protocol requires we remove them from the scene, so I gathered the equipment in my arms as I went.

Halfway across the field, I looked to my right and saw a sergeant who also had his arms full, but he wasn't carrying sensitive items. He was weighed down with body parts. Guilt crashed down on me. I, the officer who was supposed to lead by example, was protecting equipment. He, the enlisted man, was gathering our fallen soldiers' lost limbs. His was the important work. The men mattered so much more than my radios and tracking devices. I didn't know it at the time, but that moment would stay with me forever.

Taking the Mosque

In time, we found all of the men. Five were dead. We secured them, the sensitive equipment, and the vehicles, and we prepared to return to base. I stood next to the recovery vehicle, a large, armored semi-truck, talking to the driver when I heard a distinct *plink* noise to my right. I turned to see bullets hitting the destroyed Humvee. The driver wasn't an infantryman and, naturally, he was scared. He pulled away from the gunfire. As I stood there watching the semi slowly start rolling, I realized I was in the open. My squad and safety were on the other side of the vehicle, but I couldn't get to them. The semi was in the way and going nowhere fast, and for those vital seconds, I was exposed. There was nothing between the enemy and me but that damn muddy field.

Muzzles flashed from windows of a mosque. Rounds hit the ground in front of me. With each hit, the weeds twitched. I heard heavy thuds coming closer as bullets hit the wet earth. I dove behind a mound of mud no more than eight inches high and a foot wide. It was all there was. Bullets hit the ground all around me. I stayed down and returned fire. I radioed to one of our Bradleys for support, and it targeted the enemy. Their machine gun fire halted, and I jumped up and ran to rejoin the platoon.

Suddenly, boom! A massive blast rocked me. The sweeping pressure made me want to vomit. I nearly wobbled to my knees, but adrenaline kept me running. I got back to the cluster of Bradleys and our battalion commander and took stock of the situation.

"I'm going to take the mosque," I told the commander. It may have been a place of worship, but at that moment, it was the enemy's attack position. He nodded. I loaded the troops into our vehicles, and we began to coordinate, shouting back and forth over the noise of gunfire. But before we could move out, the commander called over to me.

"Mitch! I'm calling a JDAM. Get the men back. Cease fire." He told me the JDAM, a precision-guided bomb, was inbound. The battle would be over in seconds. I didn't want to wait even seconds, though. I wanted to keep fighting and suppress the enemy, but I followed commands and relented.

Seconds passed. Time stretched on and we sat waiting. The bomb didn't come. After ten minutes, the commander announced the JDAM had been called off. He didn't offer an explanation. I wouldn't have had the patience to listen, even if he had. Without a word to the commander, I began to position the platoon to take the mosque ourselves. He saw what we were doing and called out.

"Don't go in there yourself, Mitch," he said. "Take the Iraqi Army. Have them clear it while you provide cover."

"Roger, Sir," I replied.

We moved quickly into position. The Iraqi Army (IA) entered the mosque. After a quick search, the IA commander reported that there was no one inside. *Impossible*, I thought.

"Go back and look closely," I said. He did, and he returned fifteen minutes later, shaking his head—still nothing. I was dumbstruck. I had seen muzzle flashes from the mosque's windows. Was I crazy? Had the pump of adrenaline confused me?

As I paced back and forth, thinking it through, something glinted in the corner of my eye. I walked over and found a chunk of metal about six inches in diameter, weighing about a pound. It was part of the destroyed Humvee. I looked back across the muddy field to the crater—the only sign now left of the deadly attack, since the other men had moved out. This piece of metal must've flown a hundred yards. I was awed.

As the adrenaline fell away, the battle fog lifted, and my thoughts became clearer. There *had* been gunfire coming from the mosque. The mosque was clear when the IA went in. That meant the bad guys got away while we were waiting for the bomb that never came.

Back at base, I joined the other leaders in the command post. It was quiet. There was none of the usual chatter. No one spoke except in hushed voices. It felt like a wake. In some ways, it was. I was debriefing the commander on our part of the mission when another platoon leader walked in. It was his men who had died. I didn't know him well, but when our eyes met, I reached out and hugged him. As we embraced, he wept.

The Five

That evening, I discovered more about the five dead men. One was twenty-six-years-old and from California. Friends said he was a teddy bear, as nice as they come. A strait-laced, book-smart guy, he could get drunk on one beer. He held the highest standards and took pride in his work.

The next was a big Texan guy with a big drawl to match. At thirty-seven, he was even older than me. The soldiers would tease that they'd found his walker on the battlefield, or that he was a veteran of the Spanish-American war of 1898. He entertained the men with jokes of his own, often and at length.

From Georgia was a twenty-one-year-old known for his generosity. He'd be the first to lend you his car or help out with money. He was always joking but, being intelligent as he was, his one-liners would sometimes go over people's heads.

Another twenty-one-year-old was from Oregon. He was the newest platoon member and told the others he wanted to be on the ground and make a difference. A friend laughed that, despite being the platoon's resident computer expert and incredibly smart, he was the worst driver he'd ever seen.

Then there was the youngest to die that day, at just twenty-years-old. He was newly married. He was also from California, where he'd passed up a college baseball scholarship to join the Army. A fellow platoon member said, "If we had an army full of soldiers like [him], we could win the war easily." He was an excellent soldier. They all were.

Something Had to Change

I didn't know which one of them I lifted into that body bag. I hadn't known them personally, as they were in a different company, but I did know what they were attempting that day. They'd been on a mission to catch a suspected insurgent leader. They worked hard, and they were on to the bad guy. If they'd had more time, I have no doubt they would've caught up to him. But they were operating in difficult conditions and with poor intelligence. And then the improvised explosive device killed them. They never got the chance to go back out and finish what they started.

Then my platoon had gone out on a recovery mission, engaged in a firefight, and lost track of the enemy. Yes, we brought our men back and secured the sensitive equipment. But we also let the bad guys get away. We had literally sat around waiting while they most likely escaped through the mosque's back door. To me, that didn't feel like a successful mission.

The other leaders and I did a good job, I think, of talking to the men that evening. We made plans for a memorial service. We spoke about why we do this work. The next day, we would be back on the streets. There was a job to do, and the best way to honor the fallen was to keep soldiering on.

I didn't want to go on the same way, though. I knew casualties occurred in war, but I couldn't stand the idea of losing more men. I didn't want our soldiers to see their brothers blown to pieces and have to gather

up their stray body parts. No one should see that stuff, let alone work

through it. And I didn't want the bad guys to get away again. Continuing

to run missions without reliable intelligence seemed crazy when the lives

of soldiers were literally on the line. Something had to change.

Chapter One: A New Battle Drill

Four years before that disastrous day, I sat on my king-size bed at home and told my wife, Sonja, I wanted go back in. It was 2004, and America was well into the War on Terror. Presidential debates were raging, and talk was contentious around our efforts in the Middle East. I hated hearing politicians tear apart the military's efforts and argue about whether the war was working. I felt a pull from deep within to help ensure the war succeeded. I'd been trained for it, after all.

You see, back before college, I was an enlisted Marine for four years. That included a six-month stint on a naval ship traveling through the Pacific Ocean, visiting exotic locations that this Midwest kid never expected to see. My service fell between the two Gulf wars, so although I trained—and trained hard—I never fought.

I had since attended college, graduated with a double major in finance and banking, and become a financial advisor. The work was challenging, and I earned a good income, but I didn't like sitting around making money while my fellow Marines struggled in austere conditions. It was an odd time in my life. Usually, I make decisions through a logical thought process, but I felt an emotional pull outweighing logic, compelling me to go back in.

A Reason to Serve

Maybe that's why you joined. Perhaps you wanted to do your part for our country. I believe every American should serve their country for a few years, in the military or, if they're not the fighting type, with civil service. I'd already done my patriotic duty when I was in the Marine Corps, so the sense of duty wasn't why I wanted back in. It was more an awareness that I was trained and capable, so I should help. If I saw someone stranded on the side of a road with a flat tire, I'd stop and help. Why? Because, if you know how to change a tire, it's the right thing to do. I know how to defend our country, so I should step up when it needs defending. It's the right thing to do.

You might also feel, like me, that we have a duty to share democracy with the world. Totalitarianism falls apart every time, but democracy has never failed. Maybe you want to serve because you recognize that the next generation of Saddam Husseins and Osama Bin Ladens are just ruthless. When I eventually became an infantry platoon leader, I spoke to Iraqis who told me of the atrocities Saddam Hussein committed against his own people. It was appalling. He may be gone now but, as you know, other radicals have risen to power and twisted their faith to "justify" attacking without provocation. It is noble to fight against these people.

I had one more reason to go back in. I was arrogant enough to think I was needed. (Hey, at least I can admit it.) I know there are others just as capable as me, and many even more so. I always thought I was a good Marine, though, and that the men needed me. Whatever your specific situation, we all share a deep drive to defend our country and do our part, and that was the feeling I couldn't escape back in 2004.

Thanks to a Marine recruiter who hung up on me, an Army guy happy to accept anyone with a heartbeat, failing to graduate from ranger school, and getting selected to lead a platoon anyway—all of which I'll tell you about later—it was the end of 2007 before I was deployed to Mosul, Iraq as an infantry platoon leader.

Enter Stage IV

In late 2007, the world was a very different place from today. The first iPhone had only just been released. Most of us didn't know what a recession looked like. George W. Bush was president and commander in chief of the armed forces. Earlier that year, he promised to send more than twenty thousand additional troops to surge on Iraq. The Surge, as it came to be known, was intended to speed the transition of power to the Iraqi Army. We were supposed to win the hearts and minds of the locals, so we could help them secure their own country.

As I would soon discover, preparing to transition power is a really challenging phase of war that we, as a country, have struggled with. In earlier stages of a war, the strategy is simple. Politicians talk in circles for a while, then the military is sent in. We roll up and fight the bad guys force-on-force. They have tanks; we have tanks. They shoot; we shoot. We close with and destroy the enemy. We don't talk to anybody.

Most of that fighting is done in the phase of war we call Stage III: Dominate. It's what you see in the movies, and what our friends and families picture when they imagine a war zone. You may be sent into a Stage III situation, but there's a good chance you'll be deployed into a

Stage IV: Stability Operations mission. Stage IV requires we stabilize the area so the locals can protect and rule themselves. It's what we were doing in Iraq in 2007, and it's why The Surge, with little ol' me among those twenty thousand troops.

We needed all those boots on the ground as we knew no other way to win Stage IV. I mean, we didn't even have a Stage IV defined in our manuals until around that time. This type of fight was new to us. As is often the case with new and complicated challenges, we were terrible at it. We had a hard time thinking through stability operations and defining an end-state. We still do. In previous wars, it was easy to know what winning would look like. In World War II, we fought country-on-country, force-on-force, Nazis on Allies. Winning required we destroy the Nazi ideology and movement. Then, their forces would crumble.

But with modern, Stage IV: Stability Operations, we were countering an insurgency, and that looks very different. The Nazis wore uniforms; you could *see* who the bad guys were on the battlefield. Insurgents don't have uniforms. They look like every civilian surrounding them. And insurgent groups are not recognized countries. They're terrorist organizations and rogue actors operating in unstable regions with a leadership vacuum.

Battles with them are not fought on isolated fields full of poppies, but in cities packed with innocent people. This is warfare evolved.

So, where does that leave us? We can't just carpet bomb those cities. Carpet bombs are bad. More than any other time in history, we're left relying on intelligence to counter insurgencies. Local populations are vital to gathering the kind of intel that can lead to victory. Those people may or may not support the insurgents (those I met in Mosul generally didn't). Either way, we can no longer look at them as a nuisance or hindrance. We can't ignore them. And we know pointing guns down their throats doesn't result in reliable intelligence—as I'll talk about later in this book.

To win wars, then, we must engage the local population in conversation. We must use words as much as weapons. It doesn't matter if we're in Iraq, Afghanistan, or anywhere else in the world. To complete Stage IV: Stability Operations, we must build trust with locals, so they want to provide accurate information on the whereabouts or methods of the enemy.

In 2007, when I first went to Iraq, we hadn't figured out how to do that. The counterinsurgency manual told us to go live with the locals and turn them to our side, but it gave no guidance on *how* to turn them. We'd been trained to point guns down people's throats and demand answers, so that's what most of us did. As you'll discover in this book, though, I found a much more reliable method of getting locals to talk.

More than a decade after my first Army deployment, we still haven't nailed Stage IV. This is why we stayed in Iraq as long as we did. It's why we're still in Afghanistan after almost twenty friggin' years. We have the best training in the world, but we don't train for stability operations.

The Best Leadership Course in the World

When you become an infantry platoon leader, you're put through the best leadership course in the world. Your training—which I also completed—teaches invaluable lessons about how to handle people. It teaches us something about ourselves. It shows you—and me—how to lead and motivate others. We learned how to give orders and have them followed. We learned true leadership. This is why Fortune 500 companies hire the heck out of us as soon as we get out of service. They know we're trained to use initiative and overcome obstacles. When we don't know something, we work it out. We get stuff done. Businesses value that.

This book will add to your already excellent training. In these pages, I'll show you what I did after January 28, 2008—the day we lost five good men, as I shared with you in the introduction. That was also the day I knew something had to change, as I was not prepared to put my men at risk for faulty intelligence—or no intelligence at all.

I'll share how a speech from one of the richest men on the planet changed my whole approach to counterinsurgency warfare. This speech, from someone completely removed from the military, showed me how to change, and introduced me to the tools I would need. I'll tell you how I brought lessons from America's small-town financial industry to the streets of Mosul, Iraq—the city once called "al Qaeda's last stand." Mosul was dangerous, but in democratic elections held later that year, there wasn't a single act of violence in our part of the city, and my men were awarded medals and coined for their service, presented to them by the regimental commander.

My Story, Your Battle Drill

This is the story of my service in Iraq—the battles, bombings, covert missions, and discoveries. But for you, the story contains a new battle drill. Just as you learned how to carry a rifle, you'll discover another necessary skill—one that your existing battle drills just don't cover. You'll learn to communicate with a local population, earn their trust, and get them to actually want to help you. With their improved cooperation and intelligence, we can kill or capture more bad guys, have incredible success in war zones, and bring our troops home safe. This is a battle drill for talking to people.

Talking doesn't sound exciting, I know. It's not the stuff Rambo movies are made of. You might not think it sounds macho or tough or fun. But this is what will help us win wars faster with fewer lives lost. It's what will make your service mean something, just as it did in mine.

I know you want to do more than bring your platoon home safe. You want success, right? Perhaps you'd love to receive accolades and be recognized for making a difference. You want to do more than just secure a few checkpoints. Deep down, we all want to be the hero, and that's a good thing. It drives us to perform our best. This battle drill can help you play an essential part in your war. It can help you be the hero.

Effort and Humility

You'll discover this battle drill is simple but not easy. It's undeniably simple because anyone can do it. I'm nobody special, and when I came up with these steps, I didn't know what the hell I was doing. To the best of my knowledge, I am the only person using these ideas in warfare, but I've replicated my success with my platoon leaders when I was in company command, and I've seen them work with many different leaders. They have found incredible results, and so can you.

It's not easy, though, as it takes effort and humility. There are no quick fixes in war, and this will challenge you in unfamiliar ways. As you follow the steps in this book, you might, at times, feel silly or weak. This is especially true in a male-dominated unit of type A, macho men. You will need to be brave. You'll need to stand up as a true leader. You must remember that protecting the lives of your platoon is worth going the extra mile—even if that means looking foolish on occasion. You may need to stand strong and sell these ideas to your men, or even those senior to you. It might be a challenge.

It is worth it, though. You will become a trusted person who the locals can depend upon to be fair and discerning, and who your leaders can trust to capture and kill bad guys, and bring your men back safe. I trust you will be a better person for what you are about to learn. So, let me tell you the story of how we won our corner of Mosul, and how you can win at war, too. Let's get into it.

Chapter Two:

The Thunder Run and The Warning

"Do you wanna go on a Thunder Run?" the platoon leader asked me.

"I don't know what that is," I said. He laughed.

"You'll like it. Let's do it," he said. I had just arrived in Mosul, Iraq. The unit that had been there for six months were having a hard time controlling things and needed reinforcements, so our battalion was sent in to assist. The original unit were giving us responsibility for the eastern half of the city, and they were taking the other, decidedly nicer, half. I was on a ride-along with the original platoon so I could learn their techniques and be saved the trouble of reinventing the wheel when I assumed control of the east side. The army calls this a Relief-In-Place, or a RIP. The idea is that the outgoing unit has learned invaluable lessons about the area—often the hard way—and a RIP is an opportunity for the new platoon to absorb those lessons so that they can hit the ground running.

I'd been anxious to see what this platoon did outside the wire. As a newcomer, I didn't know what to expect. I had studied the map of Mosul for hours, fumbled through beginner's Arabic lessons, and tried to prepare the best I could, but I still felt clueless. So I was looking forward to learning from this platoon as I joined them loading into four gun trucks and heading into the city.

We drove to the nearest Iraqi Police station, a concrete block building that was dark inside—despite the bright day—and smelled like fresh bread and urine. We walked through the dingy corridors to the back room, where the Iraqi Police chief sat waiting for us.

"Watch what we do," the platoon leader whispered to me. He introduced the police chief and announced I'd be taking over next week. The chief didn't seem to care. Chai, a sweet, spicy tea, was served, and a little conversation occurred.

The platoon leader seemed more excited to teach me the custom of drinking chai than in talking to the chief. Five minutes of almost-silence passed before I asked, "So, what are we doing right now?" He shrugged.

"I don't know. Kind of building rapport." Finally, he turned to the chief.

"Do you have any new information?" he asked.

"No," said the chief. There was another awkward silence.

"Okay, well, we'll get going then," said the platoon leader. We said our goodbyes and left.

Going Black

We were outside the Iraqi Police station, gathered around a vehicle when the platoon leader asked if I wanted to join the Thunder Run. It was a new term to me, but the soldiers clearly knew what it meant. They whooped and fist pumped as the platoon leader hollered, "Thunder Run!"

"Where are we going?" I asked as I jumped in the vehicle with them.

"Broadway Street," the platoon leader said. "It runs down the middle of a bad part of town. We're going to haul ass and try not to get blown up by an IED."

"Isn't Broadway black?" I asked. A road was designated "black" when headquarters decided there were too many bombs buried along it. We used a marker to literally black it out on the map. Unless you sent route clearance—a specialist unit to find and clear IEDs—ahead, you were not supposed to drive along a black road. The platoon leader looked at me and laughed again.

"Yeah, Broadway's black. That's what makes it fun."

He told me that from time to time, they would drive a black road to test their resolve. They called it a Thunder Run. And there I was, along for the ride. I was freaked out. Looking back, I wish I'd demanded we return to base. But they were in charge and, aware that I was representing my platoon, I didn't want to look weak in the face of danger. So I sat quiet in the front seat and watched the streets of Mosul race by as we headed to Broadway. We turned a corner and there it was. I recognized the road from my hours of studying city maps. It had four lanes divided by a wide medium. A voice came over the radio.

"Hold onto your hats and let's go!"

"Woohoo!" yelled another voice. *I'm surrounded by juveniles*, I thought.

We hauled ass. I clutched my rifle tight. Every muscle in my body tensed. And then I thought, *I should relax so when the explosion hits, I won't get hurt so bad.* But nothing happened. We cleared Broadway without incident. The platoon leader grabbed the radio.

"Nothing fun here, so let's head to Ford Street." And that was when we were hit. Boom. An IED exploded between us and the lead vehicle. Dirt blew across the truck's hood. People were yelling. I spun in my seat, ready to jump out and hunt for whoever triggered the bomb. I thought we'd pull over and cordon off the area, question witnesses, and look for anything suspicious—you know, everything we'd been trained to do. But the platoon leader had other plans.

"Go, go, go," he yelled. "Let's go. Faster." We fled.

When we returned to the safety of the Iraqi Police station, the platoon leader gathered his soldiers around.

"Well, Broadway didn't give us an IED but Lieutenant Hockenbury here—" he nodded at me, "—just got his CAB!" Everyone laughed. You get a Combat Action Badge after you've been engaged by the enemy, and it's a big deal to receive that or the infantry's version, a Combat Infantryman's Badge. But neither is a joke. Lives at risk just isn't that funny. I was stunned. *What was he doing out here?* I thought. *Was a Thunder Run worth risking the lives of good soldiers? What did it accomplish?* While most of the soldiers stood around looking amped up on adrenaline and immaturity, one sergeant sat quiet, his shoulders slumped. Later, when we returned to base, I pulled him aside.

"Is this how things go every time?" I asked.

"Sir, this is my second deployment, first with this unit," he said. "I have no idea what we're doing out there other than testing fate. It's fucked up. Make sure you don't do stupid stuff like that when you come in, okay Sir?"

"Yeah man, I promise. Thanks for sharing," I said. He walked away with his head down. I was left incredulous. This wasn't why I got back into the military.

The Pull to Return

I suppose I went back because of 9-11. We all remember what we were doing when those two planes hit the World Trade Center towers. After four years in the Marines, I was in my last year of college and studying long hours. Over the week that followed, it hit me hard to see all those deaths, learn it was a terrorist attack, and discover who was responsible. I felt deeply torn. I was a Marine. I had served without seeing combat, but I was trained and young and indestructible—or so I felt. I was also the first in my family to attend college and was set to graduate that year. I couldn't decide if I should stay and complete my studies or go back to the military and serve my country in its time of need.

Finally, I decided I wasn't that important. We would catch or kill Osama Bin Laden, and the military could do it without me. I also thought that if I went back in then, I would never finish school. I'd stay in service until I retired. In itself, that wouldn't be a problem, but I was proud of getting into college, and I wanted to see it through. It was the reason I signed up for the Marines in the first place. My father taught me college was the path to a high-paying job but, as we couldn't afford tuition fees, the G.I. Bill was my only way in. Its education benefits program ensured that after four years of service, the G.I. Bill would pay my way through college. It was my ticket to escape my family's financial struggles.

I stuck it out at school and graduated the following summer with a double major in finance and banking. I was set to marry my high school sweetheart, Sonja, so I got a job as a financial advisor. It was a dream gig with a great company called Edward Jones Investments, and it was a world away from the company I worked for during school. That had been an online brokerage firm enabling do-it-yourself folks to manage their investments. Staff weren't able to give any advice and I hated watching people make disastrous mistakes during the dotcom bubble. After school, I looked for a firm where I could give advice but not have to cold call and push crappy stocks on clients who didn't need them. I found Edward Jones. They taught their advisors to build trust with clients and actively help them invest their money.

The job was great, and so was life as a newlywed, but the War on Terror still pulled on my heart. I came home one day and asked Sonja how she'd feel if I went back into the Marines. She wasn't into it.

"We just got married. I don't want to move to who-knows-where and be left there while you go off to war." I nodded, and that was that. I never brought it up again. A year later, however, Sonja raised the subject.

"Do you still want to go back into the Marines?" she asked. She said she'd been praying and thought she'd be okay if I still wanted to go to war. I told her I did and phoned the recruiter the next day.

Too Old to Serve

I had a shock in store, though. The Marine recruiter in Omaha didn't want me. She said I was too old. I was dumbstruck.

"I'm thirty!" I said. "And you don't want a Marine who was meritoriously promoted?"

"Ever since 9-11, we've had plenty of officers, all younger than you," he said. After he hung up on me, I called the Army recruiter, who was far more enthusiastic.

"If your heart's beating, we'll take you," she said. So, there I was, an ancient thirty-year-old, overweight and out of shape, and heading to training at Fort Benning, "the home of the infantry." At Fort Benning's

Officer Candidate School, I barely passed the first day's physical fitness test. The required score was 220. I scored an embarrassing 221. I worked hard to lose weight and get back into shape. I got my jump wings at Airborne School, graduated Infantry School, and went on to Ranger School. And that was where I failed.

At Ranger School, the goal is to "get a tab," which signifies your graduation and, in essence, is your automatic ticket to leading an infantry platoon. I tried hard, but my body just didn't hold up to the vigorous patrols. It turns out that thirty is old for Ranger School, as well as the Marines. There are some over-thirties who manage it—the record is 46 years old—but it's tough. I was airlifted out as a heat casualty and thought my chances of leading a platoon were over. However, my leaders had faith in me, and six months later, I was sent to 1st Battalion, 8th Infantry Regiment—without a tab—to lead my first platoon. The soldiers and I trained together for nine months before deploying to Iraq, ready for war. I was thirty-two by then, older and significantly more mature than the outgoing platoon leader and his soldiers.

More Than A Presence Patrol

A RIP transition between outgoing and incoming units usually consists of several patrols, with the outgoing platoon gradually handing over the reins to the new leader, who takes a more active role each time, until the transition is complete. After the Thunder Run, though, I was not prepared to work with the outgoing platoon. I didn't want to expose myself or my soldiers to that kind of craziness again. I told my commander that the outgoing unit was dangerous. To his credit, he agreed to expedite the RIP. The next time we went outside the wire, I would be in charge. Eastern Mosul was ours to manage. I was relieved, but I also felt pressure. Now, it was all on me, and I still didn't know what I was doing.

I sought out the company's executive officer, a great man named JD. He told me to meet as many locals as possible and try to find someone who would talk to me—by which he meant, someone who would share intel on the enemy. That sounded like a difficult task, but he assured me it would happen if I just kept at it. JD also had advice for when we were attacked.

"You can't let the insurgents think you'll just drive away. They must respect you and be scared of you. When you're attacked, get to a safe spot, find the attacker, and question everyone in the area."

My commander issued instructions to meet with the Iraqi Police chief, the religious leaders, and any other important community members.

"Build rapport with them," he said. Well, that'll be easy, I thought sarcastically. We're occupying their country, scaring their children with our tanks and guns, and disrupting every aspect of their lives. Why wouldn't they want to be buddies with us?

"One more thing," said the commander, before I left to lead my first patrol. "Don't come back without some kind of information." I don't know if he was being literal or not, but I took his command to heart. When out on patrol, I was not allowed to return to base without discovering some tidbit of new information.

This instruction gave me purpose. We would do more than just presence patrols, where you're just driving the streets to remind folks you're still there. This mission gave us a reason to put our lives on the line. I am incredibly grateful to my commander and JD for knocking those ideas into my head.

The Man with A Message

With my new mission in mind—building rapport with locals and bringing back information—we set out on our first solo patrol. I planned to get out of the vehicles and walk the streets. I thought it would be the perfect way to meet people and see if they were willing to talk. I was wrong. It was difficult to find anyone on the streets. Later, I would learn that most locals were afraid to even speak to their neighbors, for fear the neighbors would accuse them of helping the Americans. They stayed holed up in their homes and kept to themselves.

We kept walking, though, and about four blocks from the Iraqi Police station, we rounded the corner and saw it: a dead man on the sidewalk. I halted the squad. We were about fifty yards out. I wondered if it was a trap. Were bad guys waiting to ambush us as we gathered around? Was the body itself boobytrapped? We used our rifle scopes to get a good look, and couldn't see any wires. I arranged the platoon to provide protection as we cautiously approached.

The man must've been in his late thirties or early forties, and he clearly hadn't been dead for long. His body wasn't yet stiff. He laid flat on his back, and we could see circular bruises around his wrists—telltale signs his hands had been bound. We turned him over. There were four small bullet holes in his back. Nine-millimeter shell casings lay scattered around him. He'd been murdered at close range, probably while bound and forced onto his knees.

I called Colonel Shamel, the local Iraqi Police chief, and he arrived within minutes. He took one look at the body and said, "Yeah, executed. It's a sign, a warning to other locals that they shouldn't work with the Americans or the Iraqi Police."

"How do you know?" I asked.

"He was one of my informants," said Shamel. The colonel arranged for an ambulance to remove the body, and, as he turned to leave, he called out to me.

"It's crazy out here, Lieutenant. Be careful."

With my fresh determination to find information, my platoon and I knocked on several nearby doors. *Did you hear gunshots? Do you know who the man was? How long has the body been there? Does anyone know anything?* No. No, no, no. No one talked. We got nothing.

I returned to the base feeling like I sucked at my job—or perhaps that my Army training was failing me. How the hell was I supposed to get information from the locals when most wouldn't talk to us, and those who did were murdered for doing so? Was it even possible to build rapport with the locals? Was I capable of such a difficult job? I was angry, too. I mean, I knew the insurgents had no respect for human life. Seeing the result of that sprawled on the sidewalk made it real. It was so wasteful.

Of course, one dead body was not significant in Mosul. The city was named one of the most violent places in Iraq and the center of Al Qaeda's activities. Within a month, I would see many more deaths. I'd be shot at by rifles, machine guns, rocket-propelled grenades, roadside bombs, and mortars. I never felt unsafe; we had excellent protection with bullet-proof vests, armored vehicles, and overwhelming firepower when needed. But the image of the single man left as a message was burned onto my mind. It was a warning for the locals: If you share our secrets with the

Americans, we will kill you. For me, it warned of the intense challenge we faced in winning hearts and minds and stabilizing the area. It left me feeling hopeless.

Chapter Three:

Munger Arrives in Iraq

"Don't come back without some kind of information." That was the advice from the company commanding officer when we took over from the outgoing unit. As our first weeks in Mosul passed, that advice stayed with me. I was determined to make our time outside the wire worthwhile and bring back some useful tidbit of information every time.

For me, being a presence patrol wasn't a good enough reason to put my men's lives on the line. Driving up and down the streets just to demonstrate we were still there seemed like too much risk for no real gain. And in our first thirty days, that risk was exceptionally high. The enemy knows you're in an unfamiliar setting and you don't yet know their techniques. They understand you're dealing with a barrage of new experiences, and still trying to find your footing. They take advantage of that. They will test you. That's what happened to us.

Every day we went on patrol, we'd drive out to an area, dismount

from the vehicles, and walk the streets trying to start-up conversations.

No one would talk to us. They'd cross the road to avoid us. If we did

corner someone, they'd clam up as soon as I asked them about bad guys.

Inevitably, our patrols were interrupted by roadside bombs, small arms

fire, or both. We'd react to the enemy and try to kill or capture them, but

every time they fell back into the dense neighborhood. Time after time

we maneuvered to where shots had been fired, and the enemy had

already disappeared into the depths of the city. The toll of constant

patrolling was wearing on me. It was difficult to fall asleep at night. When

I finally drifted off, I'd be jolted awake by nightmares replaying the action

of the day—except in the dreams, we never returned safely.

The Shopkeeper's Story

Then, one day, a grocery store owner spoke up. Now, you've got to

understand that *grocery store* is a liberal term in Iraq. It can mean many

things. This particular man—we'll call him Mohammed—ran a small shop,

no more than ten feet by twenty feet, selling fruits, vegetables, and some

packaged goods. It was what we'd call a convenience store. I walked into

Mohammed's shop with a few of my men and gave him my usual speech introducing myself and asked if he knew anything about al Qaeda.

Mohammed unloaded. It was like he'd bottled-up all these thoughts, and now they came flooding out. He told me that when a US patrol went through a neighborhood, just as we were doing now, the insurgents would follow close behind. Twenty minutes after a patrol left, bad guys would show up with AK47s, threatening to kill the locals and their families if they worked with the Americans. Insurgents would point guns in their faces and demand, "What did you tell them?" They'd smash up shops and move on.

Mohammed said the insurgents wanted to introduce Sharia Law, a very conservative form of Islamic rules for everyday life. He told us about a friend of his, who also owned a store selling produce. Outside his storefront, his friend had a cart loaded with apples, oranges, potatoes, and tomatoes. An al Qaeda member came in, gun in hand, and threatened him.

"Sharia Law forbids things that grow on trees to touch things that grow on the ground," said the man. He pointed the gun at Mohammed's friend. "If I come back and the oranges are still touching the potatoes, I'll kill you." The next day, Mohammed's friend pushed his cart back into place at the front of his store, just as he'd done for decades. He hadn't changed the display. Potatoes and tomatoes still touched apples and oranges. He was a devout Muslim but knew his faith didn't depend on the arrangement of his produce. The Sharia Law made no sense, and he wasn't about to be bullied into rearranging things for no logical reason. The al Qaeda man came back, saw the display, and shot Mohammed's friend. He left the shopkeeper dead on the street for his family to clean up.

Mohammed was enraged. He said he and his friends hated al Qaeda but feared their strength. He knew the US was strong, too, but American soldiers were only around for two hours a day. For the other twenty-two hours, they were at the mercy of al Qaeda.

"Why should we assist you, when you're barely even here?" he asked me. I made promises—the same ones I made all the time. *We're here to protect you. We're going to take the bad guys down.* They weren't real answers, though, and the words felt cheap. I understood how he felt, and

I couldn't give him a good, honest reason to put his faith in us when we were about to head back to base.

From my research on the area, I knew the insurgents had flooded into Mosul after we "surged" in Baghdad. They told the locals, "Look, we're Muslims. You're Muslims. Let's fight the Americans together and kick them out of the country." To the locals, this sounded reasonable. They agreed to help the insurgents by laying roadside bombs and attacking Americans when they could. Then, the insurgents enacted Sharia Law, which the locals found simply crazy. It wasn't Islam as they knew it. This was radicalized. They wanted to preserve their faith and the sanity of logical thought but were scared of the insurgents.

Mohammed explained that those same locals who had helped the insurgents were now turning against them. They didn't fear the Americans; they feared what happened when we left. They knew that if al Qaeda took over completely, there would be far more bloodshed. Mohammed and his friends were good-natured people caught in a war, just trying to survive.

The Life-Changing Care Package

I met Mohammed a few weeks before the January 28 disaster. When we lost those five men, I was shaken to my core and desperate to do things better, so we could speed up the war and ensure fewer soldiers lost their lives. I was determined to get the locals to tell us more about the insurgents. I wanted more—and more reliable—intelligence.

As the shock of January 28 wore off, life dragged on, and my friends and family back home continued to send me care packages. I sat on my cot one evening and opened a large, bubble-wrapped Amazon envelope sent by my best friend, Quintin. It still amazed me that deep inside Iraq, we could receive packages with smiley faces emblazoned on them sent directly from Amazon. Inside the envelope was a book called *Poor Charlie's Almanac*. It was a compilation of speeches and commentary by Charlie Munger, the vice-chairman of Berkshire Hathaway and Warren Buffett's business partner. I turned the book over in my hands. The back cover said the book had been used by investors and business managers as a guide to better decision making.

Although I'd been a financial advisor in previous years, I clearly wasn't an investor or business manager now. Still, I knew a lot about the billionaire Charlie Munger. I was born and raised in Omaha, Nebraska, which is also home to the headquarters of Charlie Munger and Warren Buffet's company. In those days, Warren Buffet was the richest man in the world, and everyone knew his name. Charlie Munger was the quieter business partner, so fewer people knew about his role in one of the most successful companies in the world. As a child growing up in Omaha, I lived in a poor home and knew nothing of the world of stocks and bonds that Buffet and Munger dealt in. I did learn one profound lesson from their company, though: It was possible to come from Omaha and be successful.

So, when I saw this book about Munger, I was fascinated. I flicked through the pages and found the commencement speech Munger gave to the Harvard Law School class of 1995. He was in his seventies at the time and told a few old-man jokes before sharing some wisdom from his long life experience. He said an essential element of his success was using what he called, "a latticework of mental models."

A Latticework of Mental Models

Imagine a chessboard turned on its side to make diamond shapes. The way those diamond shapes connect, corner to corner, is a latticework. If you followed the path of those connections, you'd work your way through the latticework. Now, pretend each diamond is a different subject you've learned about over the course of your life. Munger calls these subjects "mental models." A mental model could be accounting, medicine, psychology, economics, history, cooking, a foreign language, mechanics, engineering, or anything else. Even a basic understanding of a subject makes it count as a mental model. It's just a little bit of knowledge you can use in your life.

When you latticework different mental models together, you imagine connecting them, corner to corner. Then, you can mentally jump from one subject to another, applying lessons from psychology to the study of economics, or insights from engineering to the world of cooking. When you're stuck in a situation and your education in that area doesn't help, you can use ideas from another industry to give you a fresh perspective.

This, Munger said, was a big part of his success. When he and Warren Buffet had faced a difficult decision on whether to invest in a company, they used a latticework of mental models to see the situation in a new

way. Their competitors ran through profit and loss statements and

spreadsheets and all sorts of statistics. Buffet and Munger probably did

the same, but they also applied their basic knowledge of psychology or

history or any other subject to the situation. Those seemingly unrelated

ideas gave them a fresh perspective on what might be possible with the

company they were considering. It helped them make decisions their

competitors would never have dreamed of, and they became wildly

successful.

Learning About Influence

In the Harvard commencement speech, Munger also recommended

the book *Influence: The Psychology of Persuasion* by Robert B. Cialdini,

Ph.D. Cialdini is an emeritus professor of psychology at Arizona State

University, and Munger said Cialdini's book was one of the best things

he'd ever read. He loved it so much that he bought copies for everyone in

the audience, and gifted Cialdini valuable Class A shares in Berkshire

Hathaway.

When I read this, I thought I'd better take notice. If one of the most successful men in the world swore this was key to his success, it would probably be useful for me, too. I ordered *Influence* from Amazon. It was delivered in a smiling envelope a few weeks later. (We may have had Amazon, but next day delivery hadn't arrived in Iraq yet.)

Influence was originally published in 1984, but it's full of wisdom that never gets old. It says we all want to influence people, whether it's to make sales, find friends, or convince someone to give you something. It breaks these influences down into six areas: reciprocity, commitment and consistency, social proof, liking, authority, and scarcity. The book teaches you to use these ideas, and to know when they're being used on you.

Reciprocity is the influencing technique that works best on me. It's the idea that if you give me something, every part of me will want to repay the favor. Usually, I'll want to give you even more than you offered me. There are charities that send out envelopes full of personalized return address labels. They're like, "Here, take these free labels. We made them just for you. Oh, and if you feel like giving us a donation, here's how you can do it." I see those labels and feel compelled to reciprocate. I stick twenty bucks in the return envelope and send it off, knowing full-well that the labels they gave me are probably worth pennies. Car dealers know all about influence, too. As soon as you walk in, they give you a free cup of coffee and want to be your best friend. You end up buying a forty-thousand-dollar car because you can't say no to your new best buddy.

Of course, different people respond to different triggers, which is why there are six ways of influencing people. The best salespeople use them all, mixing up their approach based on the audience. Cialdini admits that there's a fine line between using influence for good and manipulating people. If you're a charlatan, he says, you could use these ideas to do bad things. But for us normal, decent folks, it's important to understand these concepts, so we know how others are influencing our decisions.

As I lay on my bed reading, I asked myself if I could apply a mental latticework approach to solve my problems out here in Mosul. Could I use Cialdini's approach to influence the Iraqi locals, persuade them to trust us, and find more information to speed up this war? Over the next few months, I'd discover the answer was a definitive yes. I'd also learn that it would not be an easy process.

Chapter Four:

Won't You Be My Neighbor?

I didn't yet know if Munger's mental latticework approach could help us win the war faster; I was too busy to give it much thought. My platoon was preparing to move off base. The counter-insurgency manual directs that we go and live with the locals to integrate with the community better. Frankly, it sucks. The base where we were initially stationed, FOB Marez, was pretty comfortable. We stayed in containerized housing units, two soldiers to a room, with electricity, air conditioning, and privacy. You could get naked in there, and no one would know. Well, your roommate might have something to say, but it was a quiet space that had started to feel like home. When we moved off-base to the combat outpost, COP Rock, we'd be living in a big, general-purpose army tent with a dirt floor, 20 cots crammed in together, and no bathrooms. We'd have to poop in a bucket and burn it every night. I'd done my share of shit-burning, and I knew how miserable it was. There'd be no showers, no running water, and not much electricity. The only food would be Meals Ready to Eat (MREs)—those processed food bags with a scary shelf life of about 10 years.

The previous platoon had stayed on base, so we had to find somewhere new for our platoon's COP. There was a big compound in the heart of the city. It had once belonged to a wealthy guy who was well-connected with Saddam Hussein. He'd fled to Syria and left his home, outbuildings, and surrounding orchard deserted. We cleared the compound, brought in our bulldozers, and started securing the site. We had no idea that the al Qaeda headquarters for the entire country was just six blocks away. We were moving in next to the hornets' nest.

As our people worked on the compound, I had a new approach to try when talking to locals. We were going to be their neighbors, so we would play that card. I told the platoon that we would continue to go door to door, talking to every person in that city. Now, we were in a dangerous city and surrounded by bad guys, so we couldn't just knock on a door and wait for a suicide bomber to answer. We knocked, and when the door opened, we burst in and cleared the house. Then I walked in like Darth friggin' Vader, with soldiers surrounding me. From there, things got a bit warmer. I wasn't overly friendly; this is a culture that respects strength. But I said, "Salaam alaykum. Isme Mulazam Mitch. Keef hallek?" *Greetings upon you*—the standard introduction there. *My name is Lieutenant Mitch. How are you?* I always introduced myself as Lieutenant Mitch as my last name, Hockenbury, is difficult for Arabic speakers to pronounce. With the help of a translator, I continued.

"I want to introduce myself and let you know I'm moving into the neighborhood. You might have seen our bulldozers at work next door. Here's what this means: If something bad happens to you, it happens to me, and vice versa. So, we're in this together, and I want to help us both by getting rid of the bad guys." The reception was icy. I got a lot of blank stares like I had an arm growing out of my head. Some people were curious, but it was clear they were all scared. They didn't trust me, and I couldn't blame them.

The Edward Jones Model

The cold reception reminded me of my time knocking on doors for Edward Jones, the small brokerage firm I worked for after college. I was a financial advisor for them, with my own office in Benson, a small community in Omaha, Nebraska. All of Edward Jones's branches were in small communities like Benson. The company has since grown internationally, but back then it was all about bringing Wall Street to Main Street. The company opened two-person offices on the main street of whichever town or rural area they moved into and offered investment advice to the locals.

Edward Jones was different from other brokerages because their team focused on trust. They knew that in a small town, everybody knows everybody. If you came in as an outsider, you had to overcome suspicion. As a local, you had a reputation to uphold. The only way to do both was through building trust, even with people who don't understand the financial stuff you talked about. They set me up with an office in Benson's old bank building, right downtown. It had a lush green carpet, redwood desks, and an assistant—my best friend's mom—to answer the phone and greet clients.

Edward Jones taught a detailed process for building trust when you opened a new branch. They believed you should be a member of the community and go door-to-door introducing yourself to the locals. So, I did.

"Hi, I'm Mitch Hockenbury. I'm your new neighbor," I'd say. "I just moved into the old bank building a few blocks from here, and wanted to hand out my business card, so you know who I am and what I'm doing." Usually, the homeowner—let's call him John—would say, "Oh, what kind of business do you have?" I'd tell John about my investing services, but I wouldn't try to sell him anything. Not yet. I'd just give him my card, ask his name, and wish him well. As I left, I'd write down John's name and address, plus any other details from our conversation. Back at the office, I'd write a card that said, 'Dear John, It was a pleasure to meet you today and introduce myself and my firm. If I can ever be of assistance to you and your family, don't hesitate to ask. Sincerely, Mitch Hockenbury.' I'd put a note in my calendar to follow-up in two weeks and mail the card the next day.

When my calendar alert would pop up a few weeks later, I'd call John and tell him about this investment opportunity called a bond. Bonds are a safe way of earning a bit more interest on long-term savings than you can get from a bank. They're great, but at this point, John wouldn't know or trust me, so he'd inevitable say no. He'd tell me he didn't have the money right now or needed to talk to his wife, or he just wasn't interested. I'd say no worries, thank John for his time, and promise to let him know if any other good investment opportunities come up. Two weeks later, I'd call again, and tell John about another safe bond investment. He'd say no, and this would continue. Every time I called, John and I would talk a bit more, get a bit more friendly, and it would be harder for John to say no. We'd go through this seven times before John usually said yes. Seven was the magic number; Edward Jones discovered it was the average number of times you had to talk to someone before they agreed to trust you with their money. Then, I'd get John set up with a high-quality bond guaranteed not to lose his money. As Warren Buffett famously said, "Rule number one: don't lose money. Rule number two: don't forget rule number one."

Once John invested in a bond and saw it working exactly as I promised, he would trust me more. Then I could tell him about retirement planning, savings goals, mutual funds, and individual stocks. Those carry more risk than a bond but also pay out a higher return. I had ways of reducing the risk, and now that John trusted me—because I'd proven true to my work with the bond—he was interested in what I had to say.

The process worked well, but I hated it. I struggled with being rejected over and over again before someone would say yes, and it made me feel like a charlatan. Thanks to my discomfort with it, I wasn't very good. If only I'd been accompanied by 20 armed soldiers, it would have been so much easier. I still had success there because clients knew I was genuinely trying to help them, so when I asked for referrals, they happily told their friends to talk to me. After leaving Edward Jones, though, I swore I'd never knock on doors again.

My Mental Latticework

Now in Iraq, with Munger's talk fresh in my mind, I realized the Edwards Jones model of earning trust was part of my mental latticework. It was a subject completely unrelated to war, which might improve my approach in war. No one in Benson, Nebraska wanted to talk to a door-to-door salesperson, and I still got them to open up, trust me, and invest with me. Maybe I could get the Iraqis to talk, trust, and invest their intelligence with me, too. I didn't have much to lose in trying this approach. It was heads, I'd win; tails, I wouldn't lose much. What we had been doing wasn't working, so it was worth trying something new.

I didn't explain the details of the mental latticework to my platoon. I wasn't sure it would work and didn't want to sound like an idiot. I just told them we were going back out, and this time we'd be softer. If the threat was low, we wouldn't kick in the door. As long as there weren't bad guys, we'd be friendly. We would still make sure we weren't ambushed, clearing every house we entered and showing up strong, but we wouldn't rough people up unnecessarily.

You know when you talk to a dog, and it tilts its head to the side as if it's thinking, "What the hell are you saying?" That was how my platoon looked when I detailed this approach. I had their respect, though, which went a long way. They knew I was tough—we'd been shot at so many times, captured bad guys, and always done the hard right, not the easy wrong—so the platoon didn't question these new orders. We went back out, going door-to-door with the Edward Jones model.

The Edward Jones Model in Mosul

"God be with you. My name is Lieutenant Mitch. How are you?" I started the same way as before. A section of the platoon cleared the house while three soldiers stood guard around me, rifles in hand. In front of me were a man dressed in a dishdasha, an ankle-length dress similar to a robe, his wife, covered head to toe in a black burqa, and a young boy and girl clinging onto their mother. I looked at them, took a deep breath, and launched into my new script.

"I just moved into the neighborhood and wanted to introduce myself. What's your name?" I asked the man, trying to sound soft yet confident.

"Abdul," he said.

"Well, Abdul, if there's anything I can do for you or your family, don't hesitate to contact me." I handed him my business card.

"That's the number for this cell phone," I said, waving the phone in my hand. I asked him to call me right then and there, and he did.

"Great," I said. "Now I have your number, so if you need anything, you can call me, and I'll know who it is."

"Any time I want?" Abdul asked. I nodded. He looked taken aback. I knew, in his eyes, I had an almost god-like authority. I could walk into any house I wanted. I commanded a fleet of heavy-duty vehicles and armed soldiers. I could tell my troops to do anything, and they would obey instantly. I knew he saw me as an all-powerful being. Now, he could contact me directly, but I didn't imagine he'd think himself worthy of doing so. He thought I was above him. He had no idea how desperate I was for his help.

I looked at the two children and asked the eldest boy's name. In this culture, males are prized over females, and the first-born son is usually held in the highest regard. This boy, who must've been about eight years old, was scrawny, with big brown eyes and a red, snotty nose.

"His name is Ishmael," said Abdul. "He has a cold right now," he added, almost apologetically.

"I'm sorry to hear that," I said. "Listen, because we're neighbors now, what happens to me, happens to you. If someone attacks me, it could hurt you or damage your home, and vice versa. I'm going to work to keep us both safe." He nodded, and I went on with some small talk. I asked Abdul what he did for a living, where he worked, and how old his kids were. It wasn't an interrogation; it was just a friendly chat. Well, as friendly as you can get when accompanied by a squad of infantrymen in full combat gear.

"I look forward to seeing you again," I said as I left.

Outside the house, I took out a small notebook and recorded the details of the conversation. *Male: Abdul, plumber, works in the next town, two kids. Oldest boy: Ishmael, eight-years-old, runny nose.* We continued to the next house and repeated the process. For about two hours, we knocked on doors and had conversations, while constantly trying to stay safe. When we returned to base, I fired up my laptop and created calendar reminders to call Abdul and the others the next day, and again in two weeks.

That next morning, my excellent interpreter helped me make those calls. First up was Abdul.

"Hello?" said a shy voice on the other end of the phone.

"Hi Abdul, this is Lieutenant Mitch. I wanted to check you and your family are okay and that no one came by threatening you after I left yesterday?"

"Oh, hello, Sir. No, no one came. We are okay," said Abdul.

"Great! Well, you have my number. Call me if you need anything."

And that was it. I kept the call short and didn't ask for anything. I just offered help if Abdul needed it, as Edward Jones had taught me to do with those follow-up notes. I ran through the rest of my call list and got on with my duties for the day.

Two weeks later, a calendar alert popped up reminding me to call Abdul again. My interpreter and I got to work.

"Hello?" said Abdul.

"Hi Abdul, it's Lieutenant Mitch again."

"Oh, hello. How are you?" Abdul said. He sounded tentative but not nearly as queasy as last time I called.

"I'm great, Abdul, thanks," I said. "I was thinking of you today and I realized I messed up. I remember Ishmael had a cold when I was at your home. I should have asked if I could help. Should I send my doctor or some medicine over to you?"

"Oh no, Lieutenant Mitch. Ishmael is doing much better. I can't believe you remembered!" said Abdul.

"Well, I did remember, but I'm sorry I failed you in not offering help right away. Please forgive me and let me know if I can be of further assistance," I said.

"Of course, Sir. Thank you!"

"No, thank you, Abdul. Call me if you need anything."

I repeated these calls and offers of assistance with Abdul's neighbors, who'd I'd spoken to that same day. For some, I offered similar medical assistance. For another, I offered a new soccer ball for their daughter, who I'd seen playing with an old, deflated ball in their courtyard. I made contact and offered any help I could think of based on the notes from our meetings. None of them accepted my assistance, and I hadn't expected them to. Now, though, I'd had three conversations with each family in which I hadn't asked anything of them. I'd proven myself helpful and friendly, and I could feel Abdul and the others starting to warm up to me. I created another set of calendar reminders to follow up in two more weeks.

It had now been a month since I first met Abdul, and my calendar had pinged reminding me to call him again. With my interpreter, we dialed his number.

"Lieutenant Mitch!" he answered. "How are you? I'm happy to hear from you. When will you be coming over? I can have dinner prepared," he said. *Bingo*, I thought. It had taken very little effort, and now it was about to pay off. I didn't know if I'd get any intelligence during dinner, but Abdul was finally willing to talk to me, and that was progress.

Chapter Five:

A Very Different Warning

"Allah willing." This phrase drove me crazy. I heard it all the time when I went door to door, speaking to locals. They usually said it with a shrug of the shoulders, like they really mean, "What can I do? I'm powerless. It's all up to God." It felt like an easy way to excuse themselves from personal responsibility. They could have set up neighborhood watch programs and called us when they saw someone burying an IED, but they didn't. I knew they were understandably afraid of al Qaeda, but sometimes I wondered if they just didn't care about creating a safe community. Or maybe they liked watching us get hurt by bombs buried in their backyards. I often thought we could win the war if the locals would just take up arms against the insurgents.

Then, I remembered these people had been oppressed all their lives. Saddam Hussein kept them crushed for more than twenty years. Before his reign, other regimes abused their human rights. The people I spoke to, day in, day out, had never been free. They had no grasp of what freedom could do for them. It was heartbreaking to see them waste their potential because they had no sense of what was possible. I prayed they'd one day learn to fight for themselves.

These were good people, after all. The Iraqis I met were kind and generous. One day, my platoon and I stopped at a farmhouse along the banks of The Tigris River. An elderly couple lived there with the families of their sons and daughters. There were about twenty people, all told, along with chickens, turkeys, goats, geese, and a big old cow. Fruit trees and crops surrounded the house. The couple invited us in, and we spoke at length about their family and the troubles in the city. As we talked, the wife laid out potato chips, cookies, and coffee for my ten soldiers and me. They were particularly proud of the cream in the coffee, as it was fresh from the cow. Eventually, they insisted we stay for lunch. They made a feast for the family and our entire platoon, with so much food that I couldn't finish my plate. As they brought out the food, the grandchildren gathered around. They were fearless. One girl even hugged me. After spending a couple of hours at the farmhouse, we left, and I promised to return.

I tried to compare my approach—talking, listening to their thoughts, and sharing their food—to how an insurgent would meet them. I'd heard stories of insurgents thrusting guns in faces and demanding money and other valuables. They sold the goods and used the cash to buy explosives. Those explosives were intended for us, of course, but they often took out innocent Iraqis in their path.

But even as people said, "Allah willing," I knew they appreciated what we were attempting to do. They didn't want the insurgents in their neighborhoods. They hated the bombs and explosions and gunfire. They preferred our presence because they knew we wouldn't intentionally kill them as al Qaeda did.

The Morals of Manipulation

My detailed plan for convincing locals to trust me did feel like I was manipulating these good people. I was okay with that, though. Manipulation was better than the alternative. Before trying to use Munger's latticework of mental models, I'd burst into houses, point guns, and demand information. I felt like Darth Vader, going anywhere and doing anything I wanted, always surrounded by armed henchmen. Even worse, those tactics are close to what al Qaeda was doing.

I sometimes struggled to reconcile my actions. I thought that approach was necessary. I knew the ends justified the means, but that didn't make it easier. When a raid was over, and I lay in bed at night, I couldn't sleep. There was this mental anguish that kept me tossing and turning. I was responsible for the lives of my platoon members and for those whose homes I'd just raided. It didn't feel good to force information from innocent people at gunpoint, and if they were later killed because someone saw them talking to the Americans, I felt—rightly or wrongly—like that was on me. I had to protect my platoon *and* the locals. My new, trust-building, conversational method was manipulative, yes, but that felt better than being Darth Vader. The end still justified the means, and this was a means that let me sleep easier at night.

As I struggled with inactive locals and the morals of manipulation, the war went on. Every so often, an explosion would rip through a nearby neighborhood. We'd load into our vehicles, arrive on-scene like first responders, assist anyone in need, and chase bad guys when we could—although they were usually long gone by then. We'd try to figure out if insurgents were targeting the police, the local population, or us. Sometimes, a local accidentally detonated a bomb. In other cases, the bomb was set off to draw us into an ambush. That was never good.

While all this continued, I was trying to build trust with the leader of the local Iraqi Police, a big, rugged man called Colonel Shamel. He looked like he came from a tough background, though I never asked. It was clear he commanded great respect, and perhaps fear, from his men. That demeanor carries a lot of weight in a country raised by a dictator. With such support behind him, I knew I wanted this man on our side. That wasn't something I could automatically count on. I'd heard that previous platoon leaders had tried to engage him with limited success.

It seemed that Colonel Shamel had self-preservation on his mind. He held a powerful job that commanded respect, but he knew insurgents would attack him if he worked too closely with American forces. He had a balancing act to play, walking the line between the insurgency, who were committed to being around for the long-haul, and the US, whose platoon leaders arrived promising to make everything better, only to leave a year later when their tour ended. They went home for more training and a new position, and Colonel Shamel was left to endure the empty promises of a new unit on a one-year tour. Meanwhile, he saw constant news stories showing US politicians verbally abusing each other over their plans for Iraq and promising to abandon the country if elected.

I also got the sense that Colonel Shamel had an issue with age. In Iraqi culture, a young man should not wield power. Wisdom and respect came with age. Most American platoon leaders were in their mid-twenties. Colonel Shamel was nearing sixty. It seemed he didn't appreciate being lectured by young men who, in his opinion, had not earned their power. Thanks to my stint in the civilian world, I was in my early thirties at this time. I was considered ancient by infantry standards. Those extra years gave me a little more credit with Colonel Shamel, but I was still half his age, which was half the battle in winning his cooperation. Still, I pursued in trying to build a relationship with Colonel Shamel. Despite his jaded attitude toward us, he was a local man who had clearly been around a long time. He had contacts. And he was a survivor—a guy with grit and determination. Getting him on my side for more than just lip service could only be a good thing.

The Message

One day, my company commander and I visited Colonel Shamel's station. We sat around drinking chai and catching up. Then, as we prepared to leave, an Iraqi Police officer walked in and handed a cell phone to Colonel Shamel. He took the short call. As soon as he hung up, he relayed the message to us. A local said there was a large truck filled with explosives near the American combat outpost—our home. The insurgents planned to drive it through the front gate and blow the place sky high. The word was for locals to leave the area so they wouldn't get hurt in the explosion. The caller didn't give his name, but he said he knew me, that I'd been to his house, and he wanted me to get the message.

It seemed al Qaeda had shifted tactics and were now warning locals about planned bombings. In Baghdad and other areas, former insurgents had become frustrated with the number of civilians killed in al Qaeda attacks on Americans. They turned against their comrades to try and protect their brothers and sisters. To stop this happening in Mosul, al Qaeda was apparently now telling locals when they'd planted a bomb. This would mean fewer civilian casualties. It also meant locals had access to valuable intelligence, and at least one was willing to share that with us.

I'm not foolish enough to think this mystery man was just worried about my safety. If I'd been to his house, he likely lived in our neighborhood, which was where I'd focused our trust-building tactics. So, the bomb was outside his home as much as mine. I'm sure he didn't want his property damaged. However much this call was motivated by self-preservation, the fact remained: he called. He trusted I would listen to his message and take him seriously. I did, and so did Colonel Shamel.

We both knew that vehicle-borne improvised explosive devices, which we called VBIEDs, were the scariest bombs. They're usually planted in sedans, and you can get hundreds of pounds of explosives in a car. This bomb was apparently in a truck. If it crashed through our front gate, it would likely take out the two soldiers standing guard, and who knows what else.

VBIEDs could be triggered by a command wire, which is a thin wire that runs from the explosive to someone hidden with a detonator. The wire was usually hidden in grass or buried a few inches under the ground. The bomber would press a button when he saw his target come close and kill them. They could also be detonated by remote control. Again, this required the bomber to watch for his enemy to come close.

The big ones, though, were always triggered by suicide bombers. They were important attacks for al Qaeda which they needed to work. Too much money, time, and explosives went into them to risk failure from poor wiring or a dodgy remote control connection. There was no shortage of suicide bombers for these big attacks. At one point, we found a ledger book in a border town near Mosul. It contained enlistment details for new al Qaeda recruits entering the country. It included their names, hometowns, and previous jobs. It also documented their answers to the question, "What job are you looking for?" The most common response was "martyr." These men traveled thousands of miles to blow themselves up. That's a dedicated army. One of these wanna-be martyrs would get in a vehicle loaded with bombs and have their hands tied to the steering wheel. The bomb's detonator would also be tied to the wheel. That way, if the martyr got shot as he approached his target, he could easily press the detonator button with his last breath and take out anyone within range.

Search and Discovery

We immediately set off to find the truck filled with explosives. The caller hadn't given an address. He just said it was near our command outpost. We set up an outer cordon two blocks around and began to search. Within fifteen minutes, we located a truck about the size of a medium U-Haul. Instead of a box, though, it had a flatbed with rails around the sides and fabric covering it. We couldn't see anyone inside the cab, a suicide bomber could have been lying on the floor. It was impossible to see in the bed of the truck.

As soon as we identified the suspicious truck, I took up a position with Colonel Shamel in the courtyard of a house about thirty yards away. The Iraqi Police were not comfortable here. They began to freak out. I heard mutterings.

"We've got to get the hell away from this thing," someone said. I wasn't worried, though. When you have eyes on a potential bomb, there's always some danger. But we were behind a brick wall at a safe distance. If we moved further back, we wouldn't be able to secure the vehicle. We'd lose control of the situation.

I thought of previous IED attacks. Our Bradleys had been hit by anything from forty to one hundred pounds of explosives, and mostly escaped damage-free. This truck was bigger than the usual sedan used for

VBIEDs, so perhaps it contained a larger-than-usual bomb. I wondered how much damage a couple of hundred pounds of explosives could do.

Walking up to a possible car bomb is not the preferred method of confirming a situation. An insurgent could be watching, ready to push the trigger when an American comes within reach. As my company commander and I discussed calling in EOD, the Explosive Ordnance Disposal team, Colonel Shamel already had another plan underway. One of his men was hurriedly dressing in a hijab, the dress and headscarf worn by Iraqi women. The policeman, now fully disguised as a woman, approached the truck. He peered in the cab, then walked to the truck's tailgate, looked nervously around, and quickly lifted the corner of the cover. He took one glimpse and came streaking back toward us, yelling something in Arabic.

My translator grabbed my arm. "Sir, we have to get back," he said, as he staggered away. "He says there's a lot of bombs in there." I stood my ground, along with Colonel Shamel. We needed a proper report, not panicked yelling. The policeman took a few deep breaths and filled us in. There was a detonator taped to the steering wheel. This meant it was intended to be used by a suicide bomber. The truck bed was filled with barrels with detonator cords feeding into them. Through my translator, I asked how big the barrels were, and he held his arms out to show me. It looked like they were the fifty-five-gallon variety.

"How many?" I asked.

"A lot," he said. "I didn't count. I saw at least two, and I ran." I didn't know how much explosives weighed, but I did some quick math based on water. One gallon of water weighs eight pounds. A fifty-five-gallon drum would weigh 440 pounds. With at least two drums, that was almost 900 pounds. That was a lot.

The Estimate

"Get EOD out here now," I commanded. I moved our platoon back and started to secure a 360-degree area so that no civilians would be in danger. It was a frustrating task. Even with the Iraqi Police support, we still didn't have enough people to create a secure cordon. We did our best, though, while waiting for EOD. They always take a long time to show up. When they finally arrived, they sent a robot over to the truck. Through its onboard camera, they saw the bomb was command-detonated from the steering wheel, meaning an insurgent couldn't remotely detonate it.

With much effort, they eventually managed to get a look inside the truck bed.

"You guys need to get way back!" said a voice over the radio.

"How far?" I asked. We were about thirty yards out, and I didn't know how much further back we could get while still keeping eyes on the truck. If EOD wanted us one hundred yards out, for example, it would be difficult to secure the situation. There was silence on the radio. Next to me, my commander laughed.

"They're probably busting out their calculators," he said. Two full minutes later, the EOD guy piped up. He sounded uneasy.

"You need to be a mile and a half away for a minimum safe distance."

"A mile and a half?" I said. I looked up at the truck. I could've thrown a pebble and hit it from where I was. In my mind's eye, I pictured a map of the area and drew a circle a mile and a half around us. That was an enormous area.

"Yeah, umm, we estimate there are 5,500 pounds of explosives in there," said the EOD guy. Holy crap, I thought. That was about the size of the bomb that took out Oklahoma City back in '95. That blast killed 168 people and injured almost 700 more. It destroyed a reinforced concrete building. The damage spread throughout a sixteen-block radius. If this bomb went off by our command outpost, it was hard to imagine more than a lucky few surviving. We'd be dead. The company would be decimated, losing two-thirds of its soldiers. We'd be combat ineffective. There'd be serious repercussions throughout the battalion.

We fell back. Over many hours, the EOD made valiant efforts to deactivate the bomb, but it could not be done. In the end, two brave men drove the truck out to the desert, where they safely detonated it. When they drove on out, my platoon and I turned in. We'd been on patrol for seventeen hours, and the extended tension left us exhausted. I collapsed into bed and immediately fell asleep. Hours later, I woke up groggy, with the hazy light of early morning pouring into the room. I walked into the hallway, where I found a team leader on guard duty.

"Good morning, Sir. Hell of a night, huh," he said.

"Yeah. Did they ever blow up the truck?" I asked. He looked at me incredulously.

"Are you serious? Sir, look at the floor." I looked down. Broken glass covered the rough floorboards. The windows had been blown in.

"Did you see it?" I asked him.

"Hell yes, Sir. We were looking out to the southeast when they called a sixty-second warning on the radio. We were just wondering if we'd see it when whoosh! A massive light. It looked like Hiroshima. The glass blew out, and doors slammed open."

"Everyone okay?" I asked.

"No one was hurt," he confirmed.

A Glimmer of Hope

My first warning in Iraq had been from the insurgents when they left that dead body on the sidewalk. Now, a local had sent us a very different warning, and it saved us from disaster. Without that tip-off, the war would've been over for us. I'd been knocking on doors and making friends with locals for months at this point, with no idea if my crazy plan was working. Now I had hope I was doing things right. That man, whoever he was, called the Iraqi Police station to get a message to me. He asked for

Lieutenant Mitch. Sure, he didn't want his home damaged, but he didn't

just take his family and hide. He felt safe to speak up more than he was

intimidated by the insurgents. I got up that morning and saw the sunlight

because I'd talked to that man, treated him well, and earned his trust.

Chapter Six: The Canal Street Loss

One success does not win a war. I had found a local who was willing to share useful, reliable intelligence with us, but I was about to be reminded of how far we had to go in securing democracy in Iraq.

One morning, I sat at my rickety desk in the command post, going over the area maps and deciding where to knock on doors next. My company commander approached and told me I'd be taking the command sergeant major (CSM) out on patrol that day. The CSM was the right-hand man to our battalion commander and the senior enlisted man in the unit. He was a great guy, but he hadn't been on patrol with us before. I was concerned about how his presence would impact my soldiers. They might think the CSM was scrutinizing their performance, and get nervous and perform worse because of it. I was also worried that the CSM wouldn't be as fluid as we were. I felt like our platoon moved as one, and he might not move like us. I didn't ask why the CSM was accompanying us; I just knew I wasn't excited about it.

I didn't like taking outsiders on patrol. Occasionally, the company commander asked me to take out new platoon leaders and show them the ropes, and it always made me feel anxious. As far as I knew, no one else was talking to locals and trying to earn their trust. I did things differently, and I didn't want outsiders talking about my wacky techniques. If it got back to the higher-ups, I might be told to stop. They might think I was wasting my time, and end my mental models experiment before I had time to see results. Above all, I was afraid of being called a fool. I feared embarrassment.

Never Good Enough

I've always struggled with self-confidence. When I joined the Army, I failed to graduate from ranger school. I didn't get a tab. I couldn't hack the physical training requirements. Even though my leaders were confident I could run a platoon, I didn't get over the shame of being airlifted out of ranger school as a heat casualty. In my mind, I was old, unfit, and without a tab. Then I had four dozen soldiers staring at me, awaiting instructions, and ready to judge my every move. When I became a platoon leader, the soldiers watched me like a hawk, judging how I walked and talked.

Our company commander didn't help with my self-esteem issues. He was a strong guy and smart with tactics, but rigid and distant. He never said, "Good job." He didn't give me any encouragement. I felt like he expected this level of perfection that I could never live up too. Often, that left me thinking I wasn't good enough for the infantry. Years later, my commander called me a great leader. He told my wife I was a hero. It was the greatest compliment of my professional life, but it would have been nice to have heard that at the time.

After almost a year of training and six months serving in Iraq, I was used to my platoon watching me twenty-four-seven. I'd accepted my boss wasn't about to throw me any encouragement. I still lacked confidence, though. I hated the idea of senior officers telling me my approach was dumb, so I didn't let them see it.

A Quick Falafel Fix

When I was told to take the CSM out, I quickly rethought my plans for the day. I had intended to continue knocking on doors and building relationships, but I decided instead to do something I'd always hated: a presence patrol. Instead of our usual two-hour excursion, we'd go to the market for thirty minutes. I could split the two squads up, sending one to the falafel stand to order food for the platoon. While waiting for the falafels, they could move out for a few blocks and demonstrate our presence, before heading back to pick up the food order. Meanwhile, I could take the CSM and the other squad, and talk to some homeowners near the market. As we were limited for time, I'd just knock on doors where I knew people were friendly to us. I wouldn't gain much intelligence, but we'd keep things low risk while weighed down by our tag-along.

When the CSM arrived, I told him the plan.

"Sergeant Major, we'll go out for about thirty minutes, buy some food to help the local economy, and come back really quick. We're heading to a safe area. Not much to worry about."

"Sure, sounds good," he said. And off we went, out the combat outpost gates, down Canal Street, and into the market. The market was an open-air space where stands lined the road selling everything from rugs to spices, fruits and vegetables to furniture, and, of course, falafels. The two squads dismounted from the Bradleys, which took up an outer cordon to secure us in the middle. One squad headed to the falafel stand and placed a large order. I took the other team and the CSM to a row of houses about a block away and knocked on the first front door.

We'd been inside the house for about five minutes when I heard rapid shots fired in the distance. I radioed the other squad for a report. They said an AK47 shot at them. They were attempting to figure out the direction and distance it came from, while my squad prepared to move in to support. They split into two teams of four, tightly stacked together by the front gate, ready to sprint to wherever they were needed. Chewy, my second-in-command, was already outside with the Bradleys. He spotted the guy who'd attacked them running south. Both squads mounted Bradleys and headed south in pursuit. As we were driving, I radioed our command post to request helicopter support. They sent the birds in and also asked the Iraqi army (IA) for backup. Over the radio, I heard the IA was sending in four gun trucks. We were going to catch this guy.

Bomb-Proof Iraqis

It turns out that the full force of two armies, Bradleys, choppers, and gun trucks might have been overkill. Before the IA arrived, we easily cornered the single insurgent, who was hiding under a fish cart. We were handcuffing him when the ground shook. An explosion went off nearby. I looked down the long, straight street and saw debris littering the ground three blocks away. Through the smoke, the IA vehicles emerged moving towards us. The bomb hit one of their Humvees, but the vehicle wasn't damaged. The soldiers inside probably had concussions but no other injuries. All four vehicles kept driving.

They were one block away when the second bomb blasted. It hit the lead Humvee. The vehicle veered wildly, and, amazingly, kept coming. It drove right up to us, and the door flung open.

"Lieutenant Mitch, you need help?" said the Iraqi soldier inside.

"Damn, Mohammed! You okay?" I asked.

"Oh sure," he said. "Just two little IEDs. We are all good. What can I do to help you?" I was stunned. I'd just seen two decent-sized bombs explode on these people, and I couldn't believe they drove out okay.

"Did you see the trigger man?" I asked.

"No. We just kept driving. But faster," he said.

"Yeah, I don't blame you," I replied. "Thanks for coming, but we just caught the guy who shot at us. We don't need your help now."

"What? We got blown up, twice, for nothing?" said Mohammed.

"I hate to put it that way, but yeah, kind of. Sorry." I felt bad as I said this. They'd driven through real danger for nothing at all.

"That is okay, Mitch. We're all safe, so no problem," said Muhammed.

"You must be a cat with nine lives," I said. It was a casual aside, and I assumed the joke would be lost on Muhammed. He spoke excellent English, but it was his second language.

"We say this!" he laughed. "We say this about cats, too."

"Well, you've got seven lives left," I said. We both laughed. I ordered everyone to load back up and return to the command outpost. I was frustrated we'd missed the IED trigger man, but at least we had the original shooter in custody. There was one less bad guy on the streets, and everyone in my platoon and the Iraqi army was alive and uninjured, including the command sergeant major.

In Pursuit

We drove back down Canal Street, past the debris of the Iraqi army's brush with death. As we passed the site of the first bomb, we were hit by another blast. It rocked us pretty good. Chewy was clearly concussed, but he powered through. Thankfully, there wasn't any serious damage to our Bradleys. Chewy saw two men fleeing the scene, and I ordered the platoon out to pursue them. The insurgents split up. I sent one squad after each man.

The first guy had a fifty-yard lead on us, but he turned into a housing community which must've confused him. He almost ran into a fence and stopped, looking left and right. As we neared, he lobbed something over the fence and took off running to the left. His moment of confusion gave us time to get close. We pointed our guns and shouted for him to stop. He knew we had him. He stopped, put his hands in the air, and gave himself up.

We recovered the item he'd thrown over the fence. It was a small, black bag with a camcorder inside. This was 2008, and cell phone video wasn't a big thing. Insurgents used camcorders to record attacks on US forces, which they then used as propaganda for recruiting and fundraising. *See how well we blow up the Americans? Give us money so we can kill more of them!* We had intelligence reports that there was an active video recording cell in our area. They'd filmed the January 28 attack, when we lost the five men. That night, the recording aired on Al Jazeera, a popular television news network. Now, we'd captured at least one member of the recording cell, and Chewy was in hot pursuit of another.

Chewy's guy was running through a residential area, diving into houses, changing shirts, and running out hoping we'd lose sight of him. It was like a bad episode of COPS. The squad was relentless in pursuit, though. After a half-hour of his cat-and-mouse game, they caught him. With the insurgents safely secured, we set off down Canal Street, again, to return to base.

One Last Hit

And we were hit by another bomb. This one detonated on Chewy's Bradley. The armored vehicle absorbed the impact. No one was seriously hurt. We saw three guys run off, and we pursued, again. My squad cornered them in a house. As we entered the building, they exited a door that led to the rooftop. They jumped across roofs from house to house. We ran around the block and cut them off. We got all three bad guys.

All told, it took seven hours to finish that patrol. We encountered eight significant activities and captured six insurgents. We never got our falafels. The CSM saw first-hand the dangers we faced in Mosul, but he didn't get to see any progress I'd made in talking to locals.

That evening I sat in the command post, filing my report on the day. I didn't feel like we'd made any progress in our time in Mosul. It seemed like we'd *lost* ground. Canal Street, where all those bombs went off, was supposed to be safe. It belonged to us, not the insurgents. If we lost Canal Street, if we couldn't travel down it without being blown up, we'd be giving ground back to the bad guys. We don't do that in the army. It would be a tactical challenge for the war and a mental setback for my soldiers.

Chewy walked into the small room. He slumped down in the seat next to me and sighed.

"Sir, what are you planning for the next patrol?" he asked. I shrugged.

"I don't know yet," I said. "What are you thinking?"

He hauled himself up and walked over to the large map of Mosul pinned on the wall. He slammed his fist on it.

"I want Canal Street back, Sir. I don't really like being blown up, you know. How about you figure out a way to stop us getting our ass kicked on this road." I saw the determination in his eyes. He was mad. He was done with getting thrown around inside the Bradleys, and worrying the next blast will kill us. Like me, he couldn't stand losing this ground to the insurgents.

Knowing Chewy

I knew those were his thoughts because, quite simply, I knew Chewy. I'd known him since my first day in our company when I walked into the Alpha Company headquarters. I was terrified. There were about one hundred and fifty infantry dudes in there, and I knew they could smell weakness. They were like sharks; one whiff of blood in the water and they'd rip apart whatever they found. So, even though I felt like a fraud, I was determined not to show fear. I walked into the platoon room and straight up to Chewy, who would be my second-in-command.

Before I reached him, though, one of the sharks reared his head. A guy stood up and called out to me.

"Hey, Sir, where'd you come from?" he asked. I knew he was asking about my military background, and I could see a Marine Corps tattoo on his neck.

"Like you, man, Marine Corps," I said. "When did you come in?"

"I've been in since 1995," he said with a smirk, clearly thinking he had seniority on me. To the uninitiated, it might sound like he was just making conversation. This was the armed forces, though, and passive-aggressive stuff was just what we did. He was trying to be the big, bad kid on the playground, taunting the new officer without being directly insubordinate. I was ready for it. I'd seen this attitude in the Marines. There, we showed seniority—unofficially—by calling new recruits "boots." If they were a young boot, we called them a "shower shoe." You know when you're in the shower, butt naked but wearing flip flops, so you don't get athlete's foot? Those shower shoes were the lowest of the low, so there was this hierarchy of Marines, Boots, and Shower Shoes.

I'd joined the Marines in 1993 which, thankfully, put me ahead of this guy.

"Well, it looks like you're Boot to me," I said. I could feel every eye on me. The silence was as loud as a mic drop. My heart was racing. The guy sat down without saying another thing. Then, into the silence, another guy laughed. He called out to the Boot,

"Damn, you didn't see that coming!" I turned to the guy laughing.

"Well, I guess that makes you the Shower Shoe," I said. And then I got out of there.

Earned Confidence

That was my high note, and I had to leave before it fell apart. I walked over to Chewy and took him aside, leaving the platoon to talk amongst themselves. I think I won Chewy's confidence in that one exchange with the Boot. He saw I wasn't going to let the soldiers pull one over on me. I was determined to be strong. I didn't know it at the time, but Chewy's previous platoon leader wanted to be buddies with everyone. That's no way to lead in combat. Officers have to make decisions that can cost lives.

When you make friends with your soldiers, you start pulling favoritism or making decisions that aren't best for the unit. It's hard to send soldiers into certain-death situations. It's impossible to send your buddy there.

Chewy and I talked about where we'd come from and our military backgrounds. Most platoon sergeants are in their early thirties, but Chewy was about forty at that time. He was short but muscular. He looked worn, like he'd been around the block a few times. And he had—he'd been in the army for eighteen years by then. He'd done two tours with this particular platoon, and there was nothing he didn't know about them. They'd just returned from war and had thirty days' vacation before being dumped back into training with a new platoon leader: me. Chewy didn't have command because he wasn't an officer, but everyone knew he could've run the platoon with his eyes closed.

Despite this, and even though I showed up without a tab, Chewy respected me. He appreciated my strength and liked that I'd been enlisted before. He had high regard for the Marine Corps. There were a couple of other former Marines in the crew, and they were built like rottweilers. Chewy and I both made an effort that first day, but the conversation was still pretty sterile. I'll never forget what he told me, though.

"You lead the platoon, and I'll make sure everything falls in line behind you," he said.

A Promise Worth Keeping

Chewy stayed true to his word. He was the kind of guy everyone takes their cue from, and his approval of me got the soldiers on board. He supported me throughout training and our time in Iraq. We were both tough leaders. We took our service seriously and demanded a lot from those who worked under us. There were eighteen-year-olds fresh from high school who joined our platoon, and it was hard for them to fall in with our high expectations. Every one adjusted quickly, though, and I'm proud of them for that.

I felt deeply grateful to Chewy. He was an excellent platoon sergeant, knew more about Bradleys than anyone else, and supported me from the very beginning. Now, he wanted Canal Street back. I wanted that too. I wanted Chewy and the others to feel safe driving down that road. I wanted them to know we weren't giving away our territory. So as Chewy stood in the command post, his fist on the map of Mosul, asking for Canal Street back, I was determined to deliver.

"Okay, I'll figure it out," I told him. I didn't know how I'd make Canal Street safe again, but I knew I'd keep my word to Chewy. And that led to a turning point none of us saw coming.

Chapter Seven: Invert, Always Invert

I stared at the map of Mosul and knew what we must do. I just didn't know how to go about it. If we wanted to drive down Canal Street without getting blown up, we had to stop planter cells burying IEDs along the road. "Planter cells" were the small groups whose sole focus was to plant these bombs. While the suicide bombers were die-hard fanatics, planter cells were more likely to include regular guys just trying to make some cash.

The unemployment rate in the city at that time was around fifty percent and even higher for young men. It doesn't matter what nationality you are—we can all understand the desire to prosper. It's natural to want to earn money and support your family. There was little legitimate work available, and the insurgency offered the equivalent of forty-five US dollars to bury an IED along the roadside. Planters didn't need to know how to make the bomb or even detonate it. They just had to dig a hole, bury the thing, and walk away. In a place where one-hundred US dollars buys a good monthly living, that was a great deal.

Digging one hole could keep a family afloat for two weeks. When there are no other prospects, and you're desperate to provide for your loved ones, why wouldn't you make some quick cash?

We might be disgusted that they care more about money than peace and democracy, but at this time, Iraqis couldn't even imagine those things. They were under dictatorships for so long that they couldn't envision another way. We'd attempt to explain democracy and expect them to be hungry for it, but they weren't. They were *literally* hungry. They wanted food, water, and shelter. They were just trying to get by.

Considering the economics in Mosul, it was no surprise that IEDs were everywhere. We were hit by roadside bombs daily. Usually, they didn't cause much damage. They'd shake us up and occasionally leave us with concussions and damaged vehicles. But as January 28 taught us, we couldn't count on that always being the case. I had nightmares about my platoon driving over a bomb like the one that killed those five men.

Of course, we'd been trying to capture the planter cells at work, but we hadn't had much success. We figured they were burying bombs at night, sneaking around under cover of darkness. For us, with our platoons of 45 soldiers loaded with heavy gear and noisy vehicles, it was difficult to

maneuver in secret at night. The city had a curfew in place from 10 p.m.

to 6 a.m., so there wasn't much noise or movement on the streets to

distract from our heavy footfalls. Instead of going out in person, we sent

drones and helicopters with infrared cameras to try and track the

planters. They weren't silent, but they were less invasive than an entire

platoon marching the streets. Sometimes we caught bad guys this way.

Often, we did not.

My Own Orders

It was time to do something different. I'd been taking orders all my

military life, but now, when we went outside the wire, it was all on me to

keep my soldiers safe. It struck me that I could do anything I wanted. I

could do things the Army way *and* Munger's way. I could partner my Army

training with what I learned selling financial products and reading

Munger's advice and Cialdini's book, *Influence*. I could work with all of it.

That thought made me feel empowered. I could do whatever I wanted to

reach my desired end state.

In the Army, we assess situations in terms of "current state" and "end state." We look at what's happening now, and what we want to happen in the end. We ask what obstacles stand between us and the desired end state. Then we eliminate or overcome those obstacles. That sounds simple, but the difficulty is always in *how* to overcome the obstacles.

I knew our current state. Planter cells were burying bombs—lots of them, and we were failing to catch them in the act. The desired end state was that we would capture or kill planters and prevent IEDs from being buried. This would make the streets safer for the locals, who were often caught in the blasts, and for us. It would also deter young guys who just wanted to make a buck from helping the insurgents. If they saw other planters being killed or captured, it would be more difficult for insurgents to convince them to join the cause. The obstacle was that we weren't able to catch planters in the act.

I thought about Charlie Munger and his advice. He said you should use your mental latticework to bring new ideas to a problem. Well, this was a problem, alright. My mental latticework included the sales tactics I'd learned when working for Edward Jones, but I couldn't think of anything there that would help me overcome this obstacle.

What else did Munger say? Invert. Always invert. Munger talked about this in a 1986 speech he delivered to the Harvard School. Inverting is an idea that plays on the work of the 17th-century mathematician, Carl Jacobi. You might remember his stuff from algebra class. He discovered that you can solve equations by taking a number from one side and inverting it—that is, moving it to the other side. When you do this, a complicated equation suddenly becomes easy to figure out. You're still dealing with all the same components, but when you rearrange them, they make more sense. I had to invert my problem. I needed to rearrange the pieces to catch the planters at work.

A New Perspective

How could I look at this differently? I could imagine no restrictions. What would I do if I knew a bomb was going to be buried, and I had unlimited resources, equipment, power, time, and authority? Would I just keep asking locals for information? Would I ask in a different way, using another name and a different angle? No. If I had unlimited resources, I'd run around like one of the cool, special forces teams. Special forces did stuff like you saw in the movies, running unconventional operations that a regular platoon like mine would never be involved in. If I could play like special forces, I thought, I'd deploy a small kill team to Canal Street. The insurgents had a habit of placing IEDs in similar locations, over and over again, so I was sure there'd be more planters heading to Canal Street soon. A couple of snipers would sit in position on that road, waiting for the bad guys. When the planters came along in the dead of night, the snipers would take them out, quickly and quietly.

I didn't have a small kill team, though. I had a platoon of 45 soldiers. They were excellent, and I could trust them with any mission, but they weren't lone snipers who could be sent off without protection. We were a team. We worked together to keep each other safe. I started to wonder how our unit could act with the quiet agility of a small kill team. If we were snipers, I asked myself, where would we sit waiting for the planters? We wouldn't be in the road. That was too obvious and exposed. The bad guys would see us from a mile off, turn, and run. No, we'd be in a hidden position. Where could we hide?

I stared at the map. Canal Street was a four-lane road with a large median separating the traffic. The IEDs had been placed in the median, probably because the dirt there was easier to dig into than the hard-pressed ground on the other sides. About half-way down the road, there was an almost ninety-degree turn where it veered from running north-south to east-west. There'd been IEDs in both sections of the road, so I wanted to defend both areas. If we were sitting outside of that curve, we wouldn't be able to see around the corner and would be restricted to one part of the road. If we were in the bend, though, we could look left and see the east-west portion, and just turn our heads right to see the north-south section. Townhouses lined the road there. If we stationed ourselves on the top of those houses, there would be no trade-off. We could observe both directions.

Keep Inverting

What other elements could I invert? Time of day. We assumed the planters were trying bombs at night—although we hadn't had much success catching them then. What if they were actually doing it in the daytime? That would be difficult for them. The area was busy with business owners and passersby. Dawn was quiet, though. Dawn would be safer, too. If someone was caught out before curfew was lifted, they could convincingly claim to be getting an early start to work. So, we could try to get in place, sniper-style, and watch for planters at dawn.

Getting in place without anyone seeing and raising the alarm would be tricky. And once we were in a house, we'd only have one chance. We couldn't trust that family who occupied the home would keep quiet about our presence. Plus, we might be seen coming or going. You can't just walk ten armed and uniformed soldiers out the door without the neighbors talking. If people saw us, word would spread that we were using that house as a look-out. The stakes were high to get this right the first time.

I had an idea to get us in without being noticed. Each night between midnight and 3 a.m., a platoon would leave the base and drive out to the combat outpost to do a shift change with another platoon who'd been on duty there. The platoon who was being relieved would then drive from the combat outpost back to base. We'd been doing this every night for nearly two months, and the locals knew it; four Bradleys barreling down the road are not quiet. They sound like bulldozers. Homeowners heard the vehicles go by, and within twenty minutes they'd hear four more going the opposite direction to return to base. There was a rhythm to our movements. The locals were used to this and didn't pay us any attention anymore. It's like at home when a garbage truck comes down your street.

The sound is so familiar that you register it in your mind, but quickly dismiss it as the norm.

We could leave the base and drive to the command outpost as usual but stop on the highway for just long enough to drop off two squads of soldiers. As soon as our boots hit the ground, the Bradleys could continue on their usual route. The stop would be fast, and the engines would remain running, so no one would notice the brief pause. Dismounted, the squads could quietly walk through the dark side streets for about half a mile to reach the houses in the bend of the road. We could position each team in a different house so that they could provide coverage for each other. We'd have to wait out the night until sunrise, but that wasn't an issue. For this to work, we just needed to get in without anyone knowing. Well, that and for the insurgents to show.

This isn't how heavy infantry platoons were supposed to operate. There were, and are, rules of engagement. The Army didn't want platoons going into unusual situations. You see, this was a time of high political stakes. President Bush was pushing to send a "surge" of troops into Iraq to squash an insurgency we hadn't seen coming. We'd been in Iraq for far too long and lost many more lives than expected. The newspapers were constantly reporting on the death toll. More than ever, the Army wanted to avoid both soldier and civilian deaths. They were reluctant to do anything outside the norm because, naturally, they worried it would result in more deaths. I knew my soldiers could operate safely and I felt confident in our abilities, so I submitted our plan for approval.

Approved

The company commander and battalion commander approved the idea to go in undercover and set up, sniper-style, in homes along Canal Street. The night before we planned to execute, I sat the platoon down and briefed them. I asked them to go over the plan on their own, study the route, envision hiding in the homes, and prepare their gear. I warned them we only had one shot at this. If we were seen, word would get out. The insurgents would know what we were up to.

The following night came. I gathered with my soldiers in the platoon area on the base. We secured our gear so it wouldn't make any noise as we moved through the streets. As I unplugged my radio from the charger and clipped it to my gear, I realized it was April 28—exactly three months since we lost the five. For the first time since that day, I felt we had a real

chance to prevent more roadside bombs. I prayed my plan would work.

Chapter Eight: The Mission

We stepped out of our rooms into the cool night air, loaded into four Bradleys, and drove out the gate. It took twenty minutes to get to the drop-off point. As we drove, I ran through the mission's details in my mind. I pictured the route we'd walk and the homes we'd hide in. I ran through what I'd say to the homeowners. I fidgeted with the volume dial on my radio.

At the drop-off point, we dismounted quickly. We jumped into the waist-high weeds that lined the roads, and just ten seconds after stopping, the Bradleys rumbled away into the darkness. We remained in place for two minutes, watching and listening for signs we'd been seen. We heard nothing. I led the soldiers out of the weeds into a nearby alley between buildings. Without speaking, we hustled down the back roads to the first house on the bend of Canal Street.

The gate to the courtyard was locked. We lifted our point person over the fence, and he unlocked the gate. Quietly, we entered the house and found a family sleeping inside.

"I understand you are scared. Nothing will happen to you. I promise," I said. "You need to give me your cell phones, right away. You all need to stay in the same room. You cannot leave the house. We'll be here for a few hours, and then we'll leave. I'm sorry, but this has to happen."

"I understand," said the father. "We will not be a problem for you. Please do anything you like." I flinched as I imagined how I'd respond if the situation were reversed. I assured him we wouldn't touch anything. It felt like a hollow promise. I didn't intend to damage his home, but I'd do whatever was necessary to get the soldiers in position and keep them safe.

The team took their places by the windows. I left my best squad leader in charge and took the second squad to the other house we'd identified as a vantage point. Staff Sergeant 'D' (SSG D) was the best squad leader I'd ever seen. He was calm, collected, smart, and understated. Soldiers respected him. I did, too, so I left the house confident he could handle whatever came his way.

The second squad and I moved out. The other house was two blocks away, but with the back-road configuration and our desire to stay hidden, it took us half-an-hour to get there. As we walked, the dark night sky turned to twilight blue. I checked my watch every few minutes, increasingly nervous that we wouldn't be in place before the sun rose. Eventually, we arrived. We entered the house just as before. I had the same conversation with the family and received the same response.

As we positioned ourselves, we quickly discovered a problem. Unless you were on the roof—an exposed position that I didn't like—it was impossible to see the street directly below. The angle created a dead space about three houses wide. If someone emerged from a side street on this side of the road, they could bury an IED right in front of us, and we wouldn't see them. I wasn't prepared to risk lives by putting soldiers on the roof, where they could easily be shot at or seen. We couldn't leave and find another house; with a few text messages, the family could tell the whole neighborhood what we were doing. I could only hope that the sound of digging and burying an IED would be loud enough to hear from above. We settled in and waited, like deer hunters in a blind. Only, these deer could think, reason, and wanted to kill us with a lot of explosive material.

Dawn Arrives

The sun's rays peeked over the horizon, and fog began to form. Through a slight haze, we saw two men walking down the middle of Canal Street. The curfew was still in place, but this didn't necessarily mean they were bad guys. Many locals were frustrated with the restrictions. They could simply be businessmen trying to get a head-start on the day. They came closer. Both men wore scarves covering their heads, with the front pulled up over their noses. Only their eyes were exposed. One carried a shovel over his shoulder. The other held a pistol. They walked right down the middle of the median, as though they'd done this a dozen times before. As they reached us, they entered our blind spot. I radioed SSG D, and he confirmed he could still see the men. They were headed towards the very house where his squad was stationed.

He needed to react fast. He couldn't make a commotion, or he'd give us away, but he had to find out what these guys were doing and stop them if required. He told our machine gunner, to follow him to the roof for a clearer view. He commanded everyone else to hold still. On the roof, D and the machine gunner bent as low as they could while still walking. They moved to the corner and peaked over the side. The men were just passing in front of the house, and then they stopped. The one with the pistol looked around, clearly checking no one was watching them. He pointed to the ground at his feet. The other man swung the shovel from his shoulder and began to dig. D had no doubts about what they were doing. In a whisper, he told the gunner to take the guy on the right, and he'd take the one on the left.

D shot first. Then the gunner opened up with the machine gun. It was over in seconds. Both bad guys lay still.

I heard the shots and immediately ran to the roof of my house. From there, I could see D's house. It was still. There was no movement, no sound. D hadn't reported his movements as he needed to stay quiet, so I had no idea what was going on.

"Report," I said into my radio.

"We got them. Two dead. We got them, Sir," said D. He spoke calmly, but I could sense his excitement.

"D, don't move. We'll come secure the area. You and your squad provide overwatch," I said.

"Roger, Sir." I called Chewy, who'd left earlier with the Bradleys, over the platoon net.

"Chewy, get back here. Set the Bradleys in the bend in the road and cordon the area." Within two minutes, he was back, and the Bradleys were in place. My squad and I approached the two dead men.

It was an odd sight, but somehow exactly as I'd imagined. One lay on the ground with the pistol still in his hand. The other had collapsed next to his shovel and the half-dug hole. I took photos to document the scene and moved in closer. We searched the men and found a phone rigged to detonate a bomb. They didn't have an IED on them, though. We searched the area. Just 25 yards away, hidden in an abandoned building, was a 50-pound bomb. We figured they left it concealed so they could make an easy getaway if someone approached them. Had we not stopped them, they would have dug the hole, retrieved the bomb, hooked it up to the phone, buried the whole thing, and got away before the sun was really up, ready to do it again another day. We called an ambulance to take the dead men to the morgue, and we took the rigged cell phone, the bomb, and the pistol back to base. From there, we sent the items to our intelligence people, and I set about completing the paperwork to record the event.

The Real Work

The first story to circulate often becomes the truth. It doesn't matter if it's gossip on the school playground, rumors in army barracks, a social media post, or a headline on the news channels. People are most likely to believe the first story they hear. Any later edits or corrections don't seem to stick as well as the original version. In the past, al Qaeda had been quick to get fake news out about what we were doing. I was determined not to let them distort this story.

I went door-to-door along the houses lining Canal Street, telling everyone what we'd done. I showed them photos of the dead men, their shovel, the detonator, and the bomb.

"The bombs can't hurt us," I said, ramming my fist on my vest. "We're bulletproof. But you and your family can be killed by them. We just made your street safe—for now. And we won't stop trying to keep it that way, but we need your help. If you see this kind of activity in the future, call me. We'll rid this place of these bombs, and we'll keep you safe." I visited almost 20 houses and hoped the homeowners would talk to their neighbors and spread the word further. Then I went to the market that ran along the edge of Canal Street. I figured if people went there to buy bread or milk, there'd be some small talk, so I told the business owners what happened and hoped they'd relay the information to even more locals. People nodded as we spoke. They said, "It's good, what you did." It wasn't much, but it wasn't bad.

Two days after our sniper-style success, I got a phone call from the team leader of the special forces (SF) unit in our area. The man on the end of the line said that for months, he'd been trying to connect two high-level bad guys to each other. They were high-value targets—people we really wanted to track. He'd been racking his brain because he felt sure these guys were connected but couldn't figure out how. Then, he received the cell phone we'd recovered. Usually, as soon as bad guys think we're closing in on them, they use their cell phone as a bomb detonator. Then we can't track their phone's GPS anymore, and the phone is so thoroughly destroyed that we can't recover any data from it. But we found this particular phone before it was destroyed, and it held vital information. It connected these two bad guys. And the SF team lead was so grateful that he felt compelled to call and thank us. We'd prevented a potentially deadly bomb from being placed along Canal Street and provided critical intelligence that could be used to take down high-value targets in the country. It felt like I'd really influenced this war. And I had no idea how that influence was about to snowball.

Chapter Nine:

The Tipping Point for Tip-Offs

The Army kept a list of the top ten most wanted insurgents. For a long time, the list stayed pretty still. The same old faces stared out from the wanted poster on the wall of the command post. I never paid it much attention. After the Canal Street mission, though, things started to change. Over the next 30 days, we repeated our sniper-style, dawn mission in different locations around the city, and we captured and killed more IED emplacers. It seemed like every time we went outside the wire, we hurt the enemy with at least one event. In four days, we captured or killed several guys the US had labeled as "important individuals," our helicopters killed two teams of IED emplacers, and we caught more bad guys and found weapons caches in two raids.

On the most wanted list, bad guy number ten moved up to number nine, and a new face took the tenth spot. Then we caught the third most wanted man, and the rest of them shifted up the rankings. Soon, the long-ranked number seven took the top spot. And we kept on catching bad guys. Before we knew it, the old number 23 was up at number five. Every time I walked into the command post, I'd glanced up at the wall, see a new face there, and think, *Oh, hey, so you're the new number one.* We heard rumors that the insurgents were fighting amongst themselves over who should replace the top guys after they were captured. But they weren't fighting *for* the job. None of them wanted to be in charge. I amused myself by imaging their conversations as they sat around cross-legged on a rug in a dark room, drinking chai while pouring explosive material into barrels.

"Dude, you've got to take the job."

"No way! I'm not doing it. The Americans are too good. I'll be dead in a week."

"Well, I don't wanna do it. Pass the C-4, won't you?"

It felt like our success was snowballing. There's a biography about Warren Buffett, who is Charlie Munger's business partner and one of the richest men in the world, called *The Snowball*. The title is a nod to an idea Buffett often talks about: snowballing. When you invest some money in, say, the stock market, it will hopefully make a profit. Then, you can add that profit to your original amount and have even more money to invest. The larger investment can get you even bigger profits, which you again add to the investment to get—you guessed it—larger profits still. In the finance world, this is referred to as compounding. Everyone else calls it the snowball effect, and that's how Buffett talks about it. Just as small investment successes snowball into bigger profits, our success killing and capturing bad guys snowballed into more wins. The Canal Street mission was our tipping point, our first big investment win, and the more we won, the more the locals had faith in us and wanted to help. It was incredible.

Influence in the Marketplace

Every time we killed or captured insurgents burying IEDs, we took photos and showed the locals, just as we'd done after the Canal Street mission. I didn't want untrue rumors to exist, so we worked hard to keep the locals informed. Of course, I couldn't knock on every single door in a neighborhood, but I'd talk to 15 or 20 people who lived closest to where the event went down, and rely on them to spread the word to their extended families and neighbors. I also went to the marketplace every week to update the shopkeepers. The locals were afraid to be seen talking to each other in case insurgents saw and accused them of spreading messages for the Americans. There was nothing suspicious about shopkeepers talking to customers, though, so the market had become the safest place for people to meet and gossip about the community. This meant the business owners had become highly influential people in town, so I made it my business to influence them. I always told the shopkeepers when we had success bringing down bad guys, and they shared this with their customers. The message was clear: the Americans mean business, so it's best to be on their side.

Visiting the shopkeepers was one of the coolest parts of the job. Generosity and hospitality are important in their culture, and they always offered me free food and drink. I sometimes felt like a celebrity, being recognized and welcomed and lavished with gifts every time I walked by. That might have been because I came armed with 45 soldiers and four huge Bradleys, but the fanfare felt real, and after so many visits, I was genuinely friendly with the guys at the marketplace. They always wanted me to taste whatever they'd baked or cooked or brewed. Sometimes, I'd graciously accept the unnamed food item, put it in my mouth, and instantly gag. The shopkeeper would be looking at me with a proud grin like he just gave me the greatest of presents, and I'd be trying to stop it coming back up while keeping a smile on my face and choking out, "Tayub." *Delicious*. More often, though, the food was delicious, and I happily chowed down.

I can't deny it; I enjoyed my pseudo-celebrity status in town. It felt pretty good to be respected and offered gifts everywhere I went. In the beginning, I tried to pay for the freebies, but this is an insult in their culture. When I understood that, I stopped trying to pay, and instead supported them by buying their food for the rest of the platoon. The reciprocity tactic has always worked well on me, but I didn't mind. I could feed all my soldiers for 21,200 dinar, which was about $21 at the time. I was happy to pay that from my own wallet if it helped build these relationships.

And it didn't feel like the shopkeepers were trying to manipulate me into spending money with them. Maybe they wanted me to buy their goods. Perhaps they were intimidated by my status or afraid of my guns. My intuition told me that wasn't the case. I really felt they appreciated our presence in Mosul. They knew we were trying to look after them, and they want to reciprocate because they were truly grateful. I honestly felt they just wanted to give back. Generosity was their way of expressing thanks.

I appreciated the shopkeepers, and I enjoyed talking to them when we visited the market. I was on a mission, though, and I had important work to do. So, I used Cialdini and Munger's ideas to deliberately increase my influence with them further. Here's how it would work. Let's say I went knocking door-to-door building rapport with locals, and in one house, I saw a kid trying to do schoolwork with pencils worn down to tiny stubs. After building more of a relationship with the family, I decide to take the relationship to the next level. I go to the marketplace and buy pencils and pens from a small store there. The business owner is grateful that I spent money with him. The family is grateful that I helped them out. They all like me more and want to reciprocate my kindness when they can.

The Tip-Offs

Between sniper-style missions and networking with shopkeepers, we were still going door-to-door, talking to locals, and building relationships. I continued to use the Edwards Jones method I'd adapted for the streets of

Mosul. By now, my soldiers knew the drill. We were a well-oiled machine, and we didn't need to rely on heavy-handed scare tactics like back before we started this method. The locals also knew what to expect. They never knew where we were going as we stayed unpredictable, skipping streets and choosing houses at random so we couldn't be ambushed. However, even though they didn't know we were coming, and even if we'd never knocked on their door before, everyone seemed to have heard how it went from their neighbors. They knew we weren't there to rough them up, so they opened their doors wide. They came out to greet us, waving a hand, and welcoming us into their homes. They spoke more easily. It became straightforward to slide into a house, check it for safety, and have an open conversation.

People began giving us tips about weapons caches—hidden storage spaces where insurgents kept guns, ammunition, and explosives. When locals discovered a cache near their home, they'd call and tell me about it. Then we'd patrol the area, find the cache, and remove the weapons. Ramadan began on September 1 that year. It's a holiday that lasts for a full month and asks Muslims to spend time in prayer, reflection, and fasting. After Ramadan started, the tip-off calls came in more and more.

We once did five consecutive patrols finding weapons caches from intelligence passed on by people in the community. On the first, we found 150 pounds of homemade explosives (HME). The next day, we discovered 250 pounds of HME that were going to be used in a car bomb. Then we found a suicide vest and some TNT. We captured a bad guy and discovered half a ton of explosives, along with initiation devices, mortars, artillery rounds, and some stuff I can't tell you about.

One time, someone from our network of locals called me.

"Lieutenant Mitch, you should go look at this little, underground bunker."

"What?" I said. "What underground bunker?"

"Go to the house at the end of my street. There's a barn in their yard. Go check out the ground there," he said. So, we did. We went at night. With our headlamps pointed at the ground, we kicked the dirt and hay around, searching for something unusual on the earth floor. Sure enough, there were three underground bunkers there, filled with ammunition, kerosene, TNT, and even an anti-aircraft weapon.

Another man called, telling us to check out a nearby construction site. He wouldn't tell me what was there, but he begged me to take it away so it wouldn't hurt his family. We went and found four barrels full of explosives sitting in the middle of a half-built room, ready and waiting to be blown up.

Another tip-off said we should go look at a field full of trash. Garbage disposal in Iraq isn't like back home. There were piles of trash throughout the city, and this particular field was used as a casual dump. I knew that field and knew it was a wide, open area. We'd be vulnerable. Anyone could attack, and there'd be nowhere to hide.

If an unknown informant had told me to go there, I wouldn't have risked it. However, the tip-off came from someone I was starting to trust. I'd been building a relationship with him, hoping he'd come to trust me. But that's the thing about relationships; they go both ways. He trusted I'd keep him safe if he turned on the insurgents, and I believed he wouldn't send me into an ambush. Very carefully, we patrolled the field, and we found a significant weapons cache hidden in the trash. The trust paid off.

No other platoon had made discoveries like this. It was

unprecedented. My soldiers and I were thrilled as it proved our approach

was effective. Of course, we weren't the only ones making a difference.

Elsewhere, the rest of the battalion was doing great things. Reports came

in of other weapons cache discoveries and more bad guys being killed and

captured. However, these results came from multiple platoons. Ours was

the only one consistently scoring hits.

If you'd asked me before I landed in Iraq, I'd have said this was

everything I wanted. We were killing and capturing bad guys, taking

weapons off the streets, and making life hard for the insurgents. But it

wasn't until this time that I realized there was something far better about

winning in war.

Chapter Ten:

Helicopter Highs, Eight-Foot Hedges, and Shit Holes

Just after Ramadan, I sat in the command post shooting the breeze with Chewy, when a boom went off. It rattled the window and shook the floor. In the distance, a plume of black smoke was billowing into the sky. This wasn't unusual. Explosions went off all the time. Normally, we'd jump into the Bradleys and drive off in the direction of the smoke. We'd arrive at the explosion site and try to spot the insurgents in the chaos. The trouble is that they look just like the innocent locals caught up in the mayhem. It's not like al Qaeda has uniforms to set their henchmen apart. Unless we saw someone suspicious running from the site, there was no way to tell who the bad guys were. So, we'd try to salvage whatever clues we could find in the wreckage and help anyone who needed assistance, all the while hoping we hadn't just been lured into an ambush. It wasn't ideal.

Now, though, I had a network of people around the city who were willing to talk to me. A soldier in one of our compound's towers radioed over the distance and direction of the smoke. It was coming from ten blocks away at the three o'clock position. I walked over to my map pinned to the wall and marked the point with a sharpie. Right next to my black mark was a blue sticker showing Muhammad's house. Muhammad was a shopkeeper who sold falafels at the local market. I picked up my phone and called him.

"Lieutenant Mitch!" an excited voice answered.

"Muhammad, are you and your family okay?" I asked.

"Yes, Mitch, but we saw two guys running down the street, and they had a rocket-propelled grenade." I covered the phone and whispered at Chewy to get on the radio with the helicopter pilots. Returning to the call, I asked Muhammad, "What were they wearing, and which way were they headed?" he gave me a description and said they'd run past his house.

"Which direction? Coming out of your house, did they go left or right?"

"Right," he said.

"Got it. Thanks, Muhammad," I said, and I hung up. Chewy passed me the radio, and I gave the descriptions and directions to our helicopter pilots.

As they took on the chase, I sat back in my chair and realized what a big deal this was. Thanks to my relationship with Muhammad, I didn't have to send the platoon into danger. I could just send two choppers out to pin down the bad guys. All those months of knocking on doors, having awkward conversations, and being patient were paying off. Muhammad had voluntarily offered invaluable information that meant I could save my platoon's energy and reduce the risk to us all. I didn't even have to worry about Muhammad being targeted for helping us. He'd spoken to me on his cell phone from inside his house. No one would ever know he was the informant. Later, I got news that the helicopters had caught up with the men Muhammad had seen running. Our guys then captured them and seized the rocket-propelled grenade.

Hedge-Ray Vision

Muhammad wasn't the only one helping us out. The locals all around were stepping up and speaking out. But it wasn't all smooth sailing. There were still bombs going off, and I still got frustrated when people didn't help. On one occasion, a small IED detonated along the roadside. It was near our COP, but thankfully, no one was injured. When I heard about the bomb and its location, I was mad. One of our good contacts, Laith, lived right there, right at the explosion site, and he hadn't told us anything. I went to visit him.

When I got to Laith's house, he came out to meet me. I couldn't hide my frustration.

"What the hell? Why didn't you tell me there was a bomb out there?" I asked him.

"Well, you could see it," Laith said, shrugging his shoulders.

"No. I don't have x-ray vision. I can't see past these hedges," I said, pointing at the eight-foot-tall bushes that ran between the road and the sidewalk lining his property. I took a deep breath. "Look, I need your help, Laith. If all of a sudden, this hole in front of your house isn't a hole anymore, you need to call me. No one's sending road construction crews in here, so if one day that hole is mysteriously filled in, it's probably because someone buried a bomb and covered it over." He looked down at the ground and nodded. I left, still mad but feeling like there wasn't much I could do if he wasn't willing to help.

Later that afternoon, as we patrolled the area, we drove back down Laith's street, and I saw something shocking. The eight-foot-tall hedges that ran along the roadside had been hacked down. We pulled over at Laith's house.

"What happened?" I asked as he came out into the front yard.

"I want to keep my street safe," he said. "The neighbors helped. We'll keep it cut short." And he turned and went back into his house. I knew most people wouldn't think much of a bit of gardening, but this was ground-breaking. It was proof that Laith and his neighbors wanted to help. They were on our side. These people who had been so repressed for so long were finally becoming proactive. The tip-offs we'd been receiving were incredible, but they were calling us to do the work. Now, Laith had taken the responsibility on himself to make his street safer. With the hedge cut down, there were fewer places for insurgents to hide IEDs, and it was easier for the homeowners to see suspicious activity. I hadn't seen proactivity like this before. It was a game-changer.

Getting Dirty

We worked with the Iraqi Army (IA) and the Iraqi Police (IP) several times a week. They were both willing to work with us and, for the most part, did a decent job. Most soldiers in our local IA were Kurds. The incredibly over-simplified story of the Kurdish people is that they're an ethnic group within Iraq who stood up to Saddam Hussein and suffered terribly for it. In the 1980s, Hussein executed an estimated 150,000 Kurds in a vicious genocidal campaign. Even after the international community stepped in, he continued to persecute them in many awful ways. When we killed Hussein in 2003, journalists reported Kurds dancing and singing in the streets, celebrating his demise and praising the Americans. Now, I was working with a Kurdish-run unit of the IA, and I felt like they shared our goals for a safe, secure country.

One of their captains, in particular, was doing an awesome job. His name was Captain **Abdullah**. I went door-to-door with him one evening visiting the locals. Every resident we talked to had his cell number saved on their phone in case they needed him. A few weeks later, **Abdullah** called me and said he'd received intelligence that there was a weapons cache in our area. He said the source was a reliable guy who'd they'd successfully used before on multiple occasions. The source said there was a farmhouse with a generator out the back. Under the generator was a hole, in which there was apparently a large stash of weapons and ammunition. **Abdullah** trusted him, so off we went to find the farmhouse.

Abdullah and the IA led the way. We arrived at the farmhouse, and by the time I dismounted my Bradley, they'd already hooked a chain from the generator to their Humvee and were pulling it away. It revealed a small hole in the ground, maybe two feet by two feet. Abdullah and I stood over it, shining our flashlights into the hole. About five feet down, we saw a dark, lumpy liquid. *Shit*, I thought. Not, ***Oh shit***, but rather, ***That is shit.*** Abdullah didn't agree, though. He thought it was more likely that someone had poured water down the hole to cover the weapons cache, and it had turned the dirt to sludge. We wanted a better look, but the holding pit was made from foot-thick concrete, and we couldn't get the hole enlarged with the tools we had. I was about to give up when I turned around and saw an IA soldier stripping down to his skivvies. He'd had enough of standing around and decided to go down himself to look for weapons. His fellow soldiers tied a long strip of fabric around his waist and lowered him in through the narrow hole.

It turns out I was right. It was shit. We'd found a septic tank, not a weapons cache. After an extensive search, we did come across a large caliber, anti-armor bullet round, which made us think weapons had been stored there before, but someone had since moved them. Despite the failed raid, I left impressed. The IA soldiers were dedicated. A pile of shit couldn't stop them. It gave me hope for an Iraqi future without American occupation.

Voting in Safety

As we moved toward the end of the year, our area had very few incidents. We'd find the occasional weapons cache, but we weren't getting attacked. A national election was scheduled for late in the year, and we wanted it to go down without any attacks. In the January 2005 parliamentary election, insurgents murdered 200 candidates and threatened to kill any voters within 500 yards of a polling station. The threats worked. In some areas, voter turnout was at just two percent. The general election in December 2005 was better, with no reported candidate deaths and a 70 percent voter turnout rate. But violence broke out afterward amidst allegations the result was rigged.

This time, we wanted citizens to be able to go to the polls without fear. My company commander asked me to gauge the locals' interest in the election and get a sense of whether they were afraid to vote. In my door-to-door visits and conversations in the marketplace, I asked people if they were going to vote. Everyone gave a resounding yes. The women were especially enthusiastic. Even better, no one said they were scared of violence. Two weeks before the election, I went to see my company commander. He was worried. He said everyone was concerned about the insurgents derailing the election.

"There won't be any problems in our area," I said.

"How can you be sure?" he asked.

"The people are telling me they're safe. There won't be any attacks—at least, not in our neighborhoods. I'd put money on it," I said.

And there weren't. Voting day came, and people lined up in the streets to vote. Security was tight. There was an almost country-wide driving ban to prevent suicide bombers from targeting polling stations. There were no incidents in Mosul. No bombs, no shootings, no deaths. Elsewhere, intelligence reports came in about imminent attacks, but throughout the day, I felt confident they wouldn't happen in our area. As I patrolled the streets, I saw people smiling and proudly showing off their fingers. Voters dipped their fingers in ink to mark their choice, and an ink-stained finger became a mark of pride as the day went on. People took photos of their fingers and waved them at us as we passed. Other cities experienced some violence, but Mosul was safe. I felt really good about that. The Iraqi Army and Iraqi Police were far more responsible for the safety than us, so I couldn't take credit for the day. I was pleased, though, that my network had given me an accurate prediction. They had a strong sense of what was happening in their community, and they shared that with me. It was satisfying to know I had such strong intelligence, and it was a sign of things to come.

Chapter Eleven: The New Normal

A peaceful election in Mosul was a turning point for the city and the country, but our work continued as usual. The platoon and I kept going outside the wire, talking to locals through the Edward Jones method, and inverting problems as they came up.

This was a world away from the Canal Street mission and those that followed shortly after. Back then, I ran through our strategy over and over again before any raid. It was like preparing for a big football game back in high school. In the run-up, you'd constantly repeat the game plan in your head. You knew what every player was supposed to do in a play, what motion they'd make, which route they'd run, where they'd step, and what they'd do when they got the ball. I did the same thing with our missions. I constantly thought about our departure time, our route, the alternate route if the road was blocked, where we'd stop, who'd dismount first, whether we'd turn left or right, how we'd provide cover, and all the details of the upcoming raid. At every quiet moment—brushing my teeth, waiting in line at the chow hall, working out, lying in bed—I'd obsess about our plan. I made the soldiers do the same thing. We practiced entering and clearing buildings over and over again. I'd watch how their footsteps landed, where they pointed their rifles, and how they communicated with each other, and give them feedback for improvement.

Now, though, we were set for another night-time mission, and I wasn't running the soldiers through their paces. I was taking out the trash. The bedroom I shared with another platoon leader had been in dire need of attention, so I'd spent the evening cleaning, tidying, lying on my bed reading for a bit, then taking the trash out and walking it across the compound to the dumpster. As I strode across the courtyard in the cool night air, trash bag in hand, I realized how relaxed I was. When the time came to go outside the wire, I'd be prepared and alert. But now, a few hours before leaving, I was doing mindless chores. Our raids had become so commonplace that they didn't demand the mental preparation they used to. I felt like my soldiers and I had reached a new level of expertise.

We still had the odd reminder that Mosul wasn't the same as "normal life." One day, I was doing the usual, sitting in a local's living room and chatting. It was a nice house with marble tile and fancy furniture. The family was well-dressed in, well, dresses. I was in the middle of a sentence

when I noticed a movement in the corner of my eye. I turned and saw a

chicken, scrawny and short, walking into the room. It just wandered in as

if it owned the place, it's tiny feet tapping on the tile floor, and no one

paid it any attention. It reminded me of a pet dog, so commonplace that

no one noticed it anymore. Then, it hit me. This wasn't a pet. It was food. I

think its name was Lunch.

The Difference

Our scores in capturing and killing bad guys and seizing weapons

caches soon caught the attention of the regimental commander. He

contacted my company commander to ask how we were so successful. I

don't think my company commander shared my Edwards Jones method;

I'd been so deep in the work that I hadn't taken much time to explain my

techniques to others at that time. Whatever he shared, the regimental

commander was impressed with our work and came to meet my soldiers

in person. He arrived at our command outpost, met with us, and handed

out regimental coins to the soldiers. Coins are like medals but presented

without the same formalities. They're hefty, medallion-sized things that

look pretty impressive.

Getting them was a big deal, particularly given the relationship our battalion had with the regiment we were attached to. There had been a lot of competition (or animosity, depending on how you saw it) between us. The regiment rarely commended our battalion. It was incredible to see my soldiers recognized for their outstanding work. That moment was better than any list of weapons seized or bad guys killed. Of course, those things were essential, but it meant so much to see my soldiers appreciated by our superiors, and for them to be reminded that their work was meaningful. That day, I reflected on how much I loved my platoon. They were the best soldiers in the battalion.

I felt like we were making a real difference. We were taking it to the bad guys. We were changing this country for the better. The locals could see our progress and were starting to turn on the insurgents. When we arrived, al Qaeda had a safe haven in Mosul. There were sometimes 30 attacks a day in this city alone. Terrorists openly roamed the streets, and innocent people were terrified to leave their homes. Over and over again, I was told, matter-of-factly, that no one goes out at night. People just went to work, came home, and locked the doors. They didn't go outside, even before curfew. They didn't talk to anyone.

But not anymore. A year later, I drove down the streets after dark and saw people sitting in chairs in their front yards, talking and drinking chai with their neighbors. Children played in the street, even after the sun set. I walked right up to one of these gatherings, and the group greeted me like family. The homeowners thanked me for securing the area, getting rid of the bad guys, and making it safe for them to spend time with their extended families.

I received the best compliment from a local guy who was part of my network. When we were patrolling his street one day, he pointed at my platoon and said, "Lieutenant Mitch, you don't need guns or any of these guys. Everyone here knows you. If you were completely unarmed, you could walk down this street, and no one would hurt you. They'd ask you to come into their home and eat."

All this came from inverting the problems and influencing the locals. It was all a result of looking at problems backward and upside-down, and recognizing that there can be commonalities between the goals of two different groups, even when they have different backgrounds and different goals. These ideas worked for Charlie Munger's investments and my fight against insurgents. It felt like a universal truth, a method of winning against any of life's challenges.

Homeward Bound

After 15 months in Mosul, I returned to the States. Another unit replaced us, and we trained them before departing. It was very different from the Thunder Run I'd been subjected to. I introduced them to the most active locals in my network and showed them how I talked to people. I knew the new platoon was in for an easier ride than I had been. For the most part, Mosul was now safe. In May 2009, one month after I left, the city reported the lowest casualties of any month in recent years. I was grateful.

I wasn't naive enough to imagine there would be no more attacks. I suspected al Qaeda would, at some point, hit with a big attack to prove they were still around and still capable of killing. And I knew the country wasn't stable enough for us to completely leave. There was a light at the end of the tunnel, though. We had laid the groundwork, and the locals, led by the Iraqi Army and Iraqi Police, were now taking things into their own hands. They were more proactive, taking a stand against the insurgents, and living with less fear.

I returned to my beautiful wife, Sonja, and our home. Having left in winter and returned in spring, the trees were a little greener now, and the skies were brighter. Otherwise, it looked very much like it had when I left. I caught up with friends and thanked those who'd sent me care packages and looked after Sonja while we were separated. I ate far too much food and watched recordings of the Miami Dolphins' last—and greatest—season. They'd had an incredible turn-around from the previous year, and I hadn't been around to watch it all unfold. I caught up on games and enjoyed seeing the upbeat predictions for their upcoming season. Away from the Dolphins, the news seemed to have more doom and gloom than ever. Despite that, I appreciated our great country every day and felt lucky to call it home.

Keeping Quiet

I hadn't told people back home much about what we'd accomplished in Mosul. While it was happening, I didn't want to jinx it. I once heard a preacher talk about superstitious Christians. He said that when things were going well, many people wouldn't speak about it for fear of tempting God into sending a trial their way. He said this was foolish. God wasn't sitting around watching the world, waiting for someone to brag about life going well, then thinking, *Ooh, you need a tribulation in life. Zap! Here's some shit to stir you up.* I agreed with the preacher. Superstition was stupid. When it came to it, though, I hadn't told anyone about our success in Mosul. Our results were unheard of, and I had every reason to be proud of my soldiers, but I'd been afraid of jinxing us. I didn't want things to fall apart before we left.

Now, I was home, and I still wasn't talking. For one thing, it's hard to describe a war zone to civilians. They think it's like the movies, all explosions and running and shouting harried commands into the radio. You try telling a civilian that you can't shout anything into a radio because it creates too much static. Try convincing someone that it's boring to drive tanks down the same old street where nothing ever happens anymore. They don't want to hear it. They ask what life is like in Iraq, but the reality disappoints them. Even the exciting stuff is hard for some people. Loved ones don't want to know how many times bad guys shot at you.

I was also thinking ahead. I expected to be promoted soon and take responsibility for more soldiers. There were plans for me to spend six months in Fort Benning, getting ready for my next assignment. Wherever I ended up after that, I wanted to replicate my success. I couldn't wait to see if other people could use the Edward Jones method in the same way. I wanted to prove this wasn't a fluke.

I did eventually become a company commander. I had three platoon leaders answering to me, and they were sent into Stage IV: Stability Operations in the Diwaniyah Province of Iraq. I ordered them to replicate the steps I took in Mosul. Some of my leaders took to it naturally and were really good at it. Others didn't find it as easy, but *the method still worked* for them. Every platoon leader saw its value and got great results. Of course, there is more than one way to build a network and influence local nationals. The steps I outlined in these pages aren't the only way to counter an insurgency with words; they simply make up one method. And it's a method that works.

Chapter Twelve:

Back to The Orchard and Beyond

Two years and four months after I flew out of Mosul, I returned. I was preparing to take command of an infantry company, but first, I was to accompany the brigade commander on a series of flights to each of the forward operating bases (FOBs) in Iraq. Our mission was to close down some of the FOBs, so the Colonel was conducting face-to-face meetings with several brigade commanders at FOBs around Iraq. I was going to five FOBs with him, one of which was my old base in Mosul. I wondered what it looked like now and how I'd feel being back. I didn't imagine I'd get to see our old command outpost, but I was looking forward to the visit anyway.

Our Blackhawk helicopter landed at Mosul's FOB, where the commander and a few escorts were waiting to greet us. They let us drop our stuff off in a private sleeping area, then invited us into their command post where they briefed us on the current state of affairs. They'd turned the FOB into a training center for the Iraqi Army. IA units came through for a couple of weeks at a time and studied basic marksmanship skills and small unit tactics. They walked us around, and we watched an IA unit conducting an artillery live-fire session. We saw where IA soldiers ate, slept, and hung out in their off time. Most of the instruction was conducted by US personnel, and IA soldiers were escorted around the base by Americans.

A few weeks prior, an IA soldier shot an American before being caught and killed. Thankfully, the man survived, but he and everyone we spoke to was scared by the incident. It wasn't the first time an insurgent had infiltrated the IA ranks to kill an American. That didn't make it easier. There was a lot of tension in the air. The US soldiers were on edge, and we could tell they didn't know who they could trust.

After our tour, the Colonel had a one-on-one meeting with his counterpart, and I was free to wander the base. I made a beeline for my old company area. As I walked, I passed the chow hall and noticed a few of the shops that surrounded it had closed. I saw our battalion command post was still in use, but I didn't go in there. Instead, I went next door to our company command post, a small modular office from where we ran our operations two years before. It was smaller than I remembered. It was quiet.

There was a staff sergeant in charge, and I struck up a conversation with him. I asked if they patrolled outside the wire. He looked at me as though I were crazy.

"No, Sir. We don't. That stuff hasn't happened since we've been here," he said. I understood. There was no need for them to patrol outside the base. That wasn't their job anymore. The mission had gone beyond securing the area. Now, the streets belonged to the Iraqis. The IA and IP kept the place safe, and the American troops assisted from within these walls.

I left the command post and walked the 50 yards to my old sleeping quarters. It looked exactly the same. I headed back the long way around, passing the laundromat and barber I used to use. Both had closed down. I looked in at the gym as I passed. It was mostly the same, but there was some new equipment; CrossFit was a thing now. I headed back to meet the Colonel feeling very strange. I'd expected this visit to give me a sense of closure around this significant time in my life, but I felt empty. It was incredible to know so much of Mosul's security had been handed back to the Iraqis. It was exactly what I'd dreamed of, but it meant that this world didn't match my memories anymore. It felt jarring.

The Truth About the JDAM

When I got back to the brigade area, the colonel was still in a meeting. I was standing outside the office, feeling out of place when a major walked up to me. He asked who I was, and we started to talk. I mentioned I'd been here before.

"Me too," he said. We exchanged a few stories of back in the day, and I made an offhand reference to January 28. He instantly knew what I was talking about. That was the day we'd lost the five men. I said that I'd been on the ground in the aftermath, and had never understood why the JDAM, the precision-guided bomb, had been canceled. The enemy had been shooting at us from a mosque, and we'd been about to move in when the battalion commander ordered me to cease fire as he was sending in a JDAM. With great impatience, I'd waited for the bomb to take out the bad guys, but it never came. After ten long minutes, the commander announced the JDAM had been canceled. He didn't explain why. We continued to work, but the delay cost us greatly, and the bad guys got away. Now, the major standing in front of me gave an almost apologetic smile.

"No one told you?" he asked. I shook my head.

"We got the command to send the JDAM in and relayed it," he said. "There were two fast-movers inbound. Then, a visiting general called the regimental commander over. They walked into that room—" he pointed to the door behind us, "Thirty seconds later, they came out, and the commander called it off. Simple as that. We were all stunned. We had a drone overhead watching the mosque, and we saw the insurgents running out the back door while we did nothing. We just watched the video feed in silence, wondering why they'd called the bomb off."

"You think the commander just didn't believe us that the bad guys were in there?" I asked. The major shook his head.

"Nah, it was the general. He was picturing the cover of the New York Times plastered with a picture of a blown-up mosque. He was imagining what the press would say if he destroyed a place of worship. And he got cold feet."

The major left me standing outside the office, feeling like I'd been hit on the head. My stomach sunk at the thought of us losing track of the bad guys because some general was worried about how he'd look in the newspapers. Then the anger rose up. I was mad he hadn't trusted the advice of the ground force commander who was in the midst of the fight. I'd spent months cleaning up the aftermath of January 28, tracking down the insurgents who got away that day, and trying to change the impression among locals that al Qaeda had outwitted us. And it wasn't just about me. My soldiers had put their lives at risk fighting an enemy who'd been bolstered by their success that day. January 28 made our fight harder. We were the ones who'd had to deal with that.

A Last View of the Orchard

When the Colonel finished his meeting, he and the commander joined me waiting for a helicopter to take us to the next FOB. I told the commander that I'd been stationed here before and patrolled the eastern side of the city.

"Tell the pilots to take us over your area of operation," said the Colonel. "You can take a look, for old time's sake."

"I can do that?" I asked.

"I can!" he said, laughing. The helicopter arrived, we boarded, and I put the headset on to talk over the internal radio.

"Can we fly over a specific area?" I asked the pilot, showing him a place on the map.

"Yeah, no problem," he replied, and we lifted off. I stared out of the window, watching the streets below. I was stunned. There were no security checkpoints. Traffic flowed freely. When we got to the site of COP Rock, my home during my deployment, it was almost unrecognizable. The towers and concrete barriers we'd erected to keep us safe were gone. The compound was again an orchard. Lush-looking trees stood in neat rows with fruit hanging from their branches. It looked peaceful down there.

Reflection

When I returned home, I reflected on what the major had told me about the January 28 JDAM being called off to save the general's reputation. My anger had faded, and I felt okay. Understanding what happened gave me a sense of closure. It filled a gap in my story. I finally knew what I'd been dealing with. And I *had* dealt with the aftermath of that day. Even without all the information, without knowing why things had happened that way, my soldiers and I had done what we could in a difficult situation. Of course, we were just one small part of a massive war, and it wasn't won from our efforts alone. It took every person serving in Iraq and supporting us back home to turn the tide on that war. I can only speak of my story as it's what I know best, but I'm aware of the enormous worldwide effort that went into helping me do my job on the ground, and helping others throughout Iraq do even more incredible things.

In the military, we're pretty good about acknowledging the great work that goes into winning wars. That's a good thing. We should recognize the successes and the people who make those successes possible. We're not as good at talking about deaths. When the enemy kills someone, we whisper to our closest friends about what happened. We lie in bed and think about why the bad guys won that round, why they were able to take one of our people. But we don't talk openly about what we could've done differently. We don't discuss where we messed up or how we could improve next time. We don't have open debates about the value of taking down bad guys versus backing off for the sake of public relations. Maybe the general made the right call on January 28. Perhaps he could see a bigger picture that I couldn't while in the middle of it. Or maybe he'd lost touch with what war is really like, and what it takes to win.

The blessing and the curse of the military is that we don't ask questions. We take our orders and obey, and that's necessary. On January 28, we listened to authority and stood down. We retreated to the minimum safe distance for a JDAM, even though we were desperate to close with and destroy the enemy. When the insurgents got away, we sucked it up, accepted that al Qaeda won that round, and got on with the job. There is a balance to be found. We must obey orders, and we must do the best job possible. Life and war zones are not black and white. Sometimes those two do not match up. That's difficult. In those times, there are no easy answers. I found peace by using my latticework of mental models to find new ways of doing the best job possible, and for that, I am thankful.

Conclusion:

Lessons from A Lifelong Learner

Charlie Munger has made a crazy amount of money. As I write, his reported net worth is almost $2 billion. That's after he's donated hundreds of millions of dollars to charity and his children. He's used his wealth to have a positive impact on his family and the world at large. He's an excellent example of a man. I have tried to follow his example in life. One of these is his habit of being a lifelong learner. Learning is a real priority for him.

"I constantly see people rise in life who are not the smartest, sometimes not even the most diligent, but they are learning machines," Munger once told a reporter. "They go to bed every night a little wiser than when they got up. And boy does that help — particularly when you have a long run ahead of you."

Becoming a learning machine led me to follow a rabbit hole of research after reading Munger's speeches, which led to my reading *Influence* by Robert Cialdini, and the other powerful books I list in the resources section of this book. I took Munger's advice to war with me, and you can do the same.

One of those key pieces of advice was to use a latticework of my own mental models to see problems in a new light. I was lucky in that I'd spent many years outside of the military working as a financial advisor, so I had mental models other than the army to be inspired by. That's how I came up with the idea of applying the Edward Jones networking method to searching for reliable intelligence in a war zone. If you haven't had the opportunity to develop a latticework of your own mental models, you can still can. If you haven't had many different experiences in life, you can deliberately expand your knowledge and ideas, and start to create your own latticework. Here are some ideas on how to do that.

First, Read

First, you must read. On another occasion, Munger said, "In my whole life, I have known no wise people (over a broad subject matter area) who didn't read all the time—none, zero. You'd be amazed at how much Warren [Buffett] reads—and at how much I read. My children laugh at me. They think I'm a book with a couple of legs sticking out."

I read more books in my first six months in Iraq than I did in the whole of my high school and college years. I never kept a record, but suffice to say that until Iraq, I hadn't read many books in my life. After six months there, though, I'd knocked through 20 books. Life has ebbed and flowed since then, and my reading pace has gone up and down with it. I've kept the habit of learning through reading, though.

Reading lets you see the world from other people's perspectives, which can give you fresh ideas and mental models. This is why your college forced you to take general education classes in subjects you didn't care about. They wanted you to develop a broader perspective than just that of your major. I'm a finance major with a master's degree in business administration, and I had to take cultural classes at school. I hated them at the time, but they added to the mental models available to me. Your college classes gave you mental models, too. You might not have thought about them in a while, but it's time to consider what you can apply from those subjects to your current circumstances.

In addition to revisiting your college reading, you need to pick up books on sales, business, and psychology. You don't need to get deep in the weeds with these things, but you need at least a basic understanding of the major concepts in these areas so that you can work with them. Start with those listed in the resources section of this book, and keep going from there.

It takes time to read a ton of books. There's no denying that. Soon, though, you're going to have soldiers' lives in your hands. You need to take that responsibility seriously. Part of that involves proper preparation. It requires you do everything possible to give you and your platoon the best chance of success. Your life literally depends on your ability to do your job well. Reading will help you do that. Army training gets you in peak physical shape, and you need to support that by getting your brain in gear. There'll be a lot coming at you when you deploy, so start reading before you leave. You're reading this now, so I know you've started. Keep going. Pick up the next book that grabs your interest. Don't stop reading.

When you feel pulled to turn on Netflix and watch mindless TV,
remember your responsibility. Choose the hard right over the easy wrong
and open a damn book.

Be Aware of Chain of Command Challenges

You must also be prepared for challenges that the chain of command
may bring. The military's chain of command is hugely important. It
outlines who you report to and who reports to you. Just as in civilian
corporations, the hierarchy provides essential structure and clarity. It
should be respected. This can be a challenge when you're trying to do
something new like I did in Mosul, and your immediate superior doesn't
support you. In an organization where you're not supposed to think
outside the box, new approaches can come across as a challenge to
authority. It's not. At least, it shouldn't be. Everything I've outlined in this
book aligns with the Army's goals in Stage IV: Stability Operations, and it
helps achieve those goals faster than traditional point-a-gun-in-their-face
methods.

My company commander never questioned the way I talked to locals
in Mosul. He was very results-oriented, and I was providing results. I am

deeply grateful for his support in that way. He was not, however, supportive of sharing my method with others outside of his company. I don't know why, and, in fairness, I didn't ask to share my method further. I had enough on my plate as it was. I got the impression it wasn't encouraged, though. When we're in the midst of war, everyone has too much to do and too little time to be concerned with new ideas.

We do a lot of things really well in the Army, but staying open to new concepts is not one of them. We want to say we're "a learning organization," but promotions come from successes, which reinforces two common and often false ideas: what worked in the past will work in the future, and what worked for me will work for you. It's natural to lean on these ideas, and, in some ways, it makes sense to learn from others' experiences. To a degree, it's what I'm saying in these pages. My method worked for me in the past, and I'm suggesting it will work for you in the future. Problems come when we rely so heavily on what worked for others in the past that we forget to stay open to new ideas. That's why it's so important to not just take my words as gospel but to develop your own latticework of mental models. That will keep you open-minded. It will let you learn from others and the past, and also find new approaches to solve your unique challenges.

Don't be surprised if your immediate superior is close-minded about how to get locals talking more. They've been raised in an organization that's struggled with this for years. You must still respect them, even if they're not willing to let you try new ideas. Don't be tempted to "jump the chain" by going to your boss' boss for approval. That's never cool— unless your immediate superior is doing unethical, immoral, or illegal stuff. It also won't help. If your immediate superior isn't genuinely on your side, they can undo any of your gains. If they rough-up a person or their property, it doesn't matter what you say to the locals afterward. They'll see you and your superior as one entity, and they won't trust you.

You can try to get buy-in from your superior by openly sharing what you want to do. Don't be shy about it. Pass them this book. Tell them your plans. I simply said that I was going to talk to people, and we would treat everyone as we would our people back home. (The exception, of course, was anyone clearly identified as a bad guy.) I gave my commander and my platoon members the same message I planned to give to the locals. I told them all that I wanted to keep people safe, treat everyone with respect, and do what I could to help. I was eating my own cooking, so to speak. This is what the Army calls "information operations." It's a branding and messaging exercise. It requires you put together a brand commercial, of sorts, to promote your idea to everyone who you need to get on-board.

This will also help with the challenge of peer leading and coaching. That's a fancy name for something most people have experienced in an off-hand way. Someone of the same rank as you comes over and says they need some advice. They tell you what's going on and what they're thinking of doing about it. But here's the kicker: they don't really want advice. They're just after a sounding-board, someone to hear and approve of their existing ideas. If you take them at their word and start offering advice, that's peer coaching, and it's not always welcome. The Army has a competitive culture, which often makes us feel like we're working against each other. This doesn't encourage honest sharing of ideas.

We're also working in situations where it's hard to tell if we're winning or not. Our only scorecard is the number of insurgents we've killed or captured, and the number of weapons caches we've found. Those things mean a lot, but they're not what "winning" is about. The end-game is stability in the country we're helping. It's handing power back to the locals. That's difficult to track when you're in the midst of it. So even if your method of talking to locals is "winning," it can be hard to get your peers to listen and appreciate the advice. Again, the best approach here is to understand when someone wants peer coaching versus just a sounding board. If they're open to it, talk about your ideas, share this book, and do it with humility.

Be Humble

About halfway through my deployment, I noticed that each new platoon leader in our company was ordered to come on patrol with me to learn as much as they could. My commander would say, "Mitch, you're taking the new PL out on your patrol tomorrow. Teach them how to talk to the people." At this time, I didn't have a defined "method," so I didn't have a set of steps for new PLs like I now have in the checklist section at the end of this book. Nonetheless, I tried to walk them through exactly what I did on patrol and on the phone from the command post. I got really into the details. After visiting a house, I'd stop to tell the new PL why I said what I did, which details I was writing down, and when I'd be following up with the homeowner. After an hour or so on patrol, I'd ask the new PL if they wanted a turn talking to the next neighbor. They usually declined.

I wasn't surprised. In the Army, we have an alpha male mentality. No one wants to look like they don't know what they're doing. This really screws up learning. If you're not willing to do something badly, you can't learn to do it better. But to be willing to do something you're not yet good at, you need to be a bit humble. You have to be okay knowing you don't know everything. You must kill the tough-guy routine. That's not easy when you think you're judged for any apparent weakness, which is how we often feel in the Army, but it is necessary to learn new approaches.

Many guys don't want to look weak because they worry it'll make them look gay. People don't always say this out loud, but for many men, it's there in some deep part of their subconscious. They equate weakness with gayness. It's sadly not surprising that in an all-male infantry, homophobia is alive and well. We're getting better with the lifting of "don't ask, don't tell," and the inclusion of women in the ranks will certainly help. But in case you haven't been exposed to this idea before, let me tell you straight: Who you find attractive doesn't determine your strength—physical, mental, or emotional. Gay people are not weak and being weak doesn't make you gay.

It also doesn't make you gay to lean on "soft skills" like talking and listening, instead of pointing a gun in everyone's face. It takes strength to walk softly. It's certainly easier to be the tough guy. You probably imagined being in war would be like Rambo, and you'd be running around blowing things up and showing your strength. And it's certainly true that if you scare the piss out of a guy, he'll tell you anything you want to hear. But that's the thing: anything *you want to hear*. And that's not usually the same as *the truth*. You'll get results from pointing your gun at people, but it's not likely to be the results you want. You'll get questionable intelligence and support for the insurgents. Everyone will fall in line, but it'll be the wrong line. So instead, be humble enough to try the soft approach. Understand this doesn't make you less manly. Keep your eyes on the end-game, even if it means you don't match the image you had of what war looks like. I'm not asking you to go soft on the bad guys. Kill or capture those assholes, but take it easy with the local population. They're innocent bystanders. Help them. They won't see you as weak. They'll appreciate your attitude and want to help you.

Prepare for Success

If this softer approach loses you some respect with more close-minded people, it won't last long. This method pays dividends fast, and any time you can use your latticework of mental models, you'll get a step closer to winning. There will be days—many of them—when you think you're getting nowhere. It's a normal feeling, but remember that you're playing the long game, not just looking for short-term wins. You must persevere. This is how you "fight" a stability operation. It's how I did it. And was it everything I wanted? No. It was better. Before deploying, I hoped, wished, and wanted to be as successful as we were, but the realist in me expected otherwise. My time in Mosul taught me that success is a real option. I learned that successfully fighting for something bigger than yourself is truly life changing. It's incredible. I can't wait for you to experience it.

How to Build Your Network and Influence Local Nationals:

BONUS! Go to **www.TacticalInfluenceBook.com** and download your free field guide which includes this checklist and script as a gift for reading this book.

A Checklist

Below is a checklist of the steps involved in building a network, influencing local nationals, and countering an insurgency with words. As you read the checklist, think through my story and how I applied these steps in Mosul. Then, consider how you can apply them to your situation.

Step 1. Meet Everyone

- Pick a street and secure the block with your vehicles on the perimeter.
- Knock on the first door. When someone answers,

- Introduce yourself.

- Tell them you're their new neighbor.

- Say you're there to protect them and their family.

- Ask if there's anything they feel you should know. Ask if they have information regarding bad people or weapons or bombs that might hurt them or their families. Don't expect them to tell you anything, at least not the first time you meet.

- Ask their occupation and the names of their kids.

- Shoot the "stuff" with them, if they're open.

- Give them your business card with your cell phone number. (This must be in their language.)

- Have them call your phone "to ensure the number works" while you're standing in front of them. This will give you their number without you having to ask for it.

- When they ring your phone, smile, and say, "Great, now you know how to contact me if you need me."

- Then walk away.

- Once outside, write down the following in a notebook:

  - Their address.

  - Their name.

- o Their phone number.

- o Their occupation.

- o Their children's' names.

- o Any other details of note.

- o Their demeanor. If they were open and friendly, they could be a future network connection. If they were cold toward you, they could be a bad guy. Or, they could be innocent and simply unhappy that you walked into their home like Darth Vader.

- Repeat the above steps with the next house and continue along the street until your patrol is over.

Step 2. Record Notes and Calendar Reminders

- When you return to your command post, use your resources to enter the information you wrote down for each person you spoke with. It may look something like this: *Father: Ibrahim Mukhtar, 74 Hay Alzirai Road, plumber. Son: Muhammed, about 10 years old, had a runny nose. Two daughters.*

- Use your calendar software, such as Microsoft Outlook, to schedule an appointment to call those people the next day. This can be one appointment with multiple names listed within it. For example, *Call Ibrahim Mukhtar, Nawaf Fadhil, Abdul Al-bazi, and Laith Ammouri from Hay Alzirai Road.*

- Create a second appointment for yourself to call those people again two weeks from tomorrow.

Step 3. Make the First Phone Call

- The next day, grab your interpreter and cell phone, and go to your calendar reminder. Call the first person, who in our example is Ibrahim, and use this script when they answer:
  - You: Good morning, Ibrahim. This is [your name]. I wanted to make sure that when I left yesterday, no bad guys came along and messed with you or your family. Are you okay? Are you safe?
  - Ibrahim: Yes, we are okay. No one came.
  - You: Great. If you need me, you call me. If someone messes with you, I will have helicopters flying over your house in five minutes.
- Then hang up. Even if Ibrahim starts to speak, hang up. This will ensure you don't end up asking for anything.

-

Step 4. Make the Second Phone Call

- Two weeks later, your calendar will pop-up with a reminder to call Ibrahim and his neighbors again.

- Pull up your notes about Ibrahim and his family.

- With your interpreter, call Ibrahim and use this script when he answers:

  o You: Ibrahim, it's [your name]. I was thinking of you this morning, and I realized I was a bad person. I saw Muhammed was sick and I was going to send the doctor over to help him, but then completely forgot while we were talking. Can I send a doctor for him now? Is he okay?

  o Ibrahim: Oh, I can't believe you remembered. No, Muhammed is fine. No need to send the doctor but thank you.

  o You: Oh, good. I'm glad he's okay. Again, I am sorry, but if you need me to get a doctor or need me for anything else, please don't hesitate to call.

- Then hang up. Don't wait for a response. You have now made three contacts with Ibrahim, one in person and two via phone, and you haven't asked for any intel. All you've done is make it clear that you are not a threat and that you want to help. This will blow his mind.

- Create another calendar reminder to call again in two weeks.

Step 5. Make the Third Phone Call

- Two weeks later, your calendar will pop-up with your next reminder to call Ibrahim and his neighbors again. It has now been a month and a day since you first met in person in Ibrahim's home. You've asked for nothing and left enough time between calls to show you're not nagging him.
- Pull up your notes about Ibrahim and his family and make the next call, which typically starts by following this script:
  - You: Hello Ibrahim, it's [your name].
  - Ibrahim: Hello! How are you?
  - You: I'm good. Thanks for asking.
  - Ibrahim: When will you come to the house again? Come over for dinner.
  - You: I will soon. I just wanted to check in with you and see how things are going.
- Ibrahim will, most likely, be happy to talk. Just build rapport with him. If he gives you information, great. If not, it's not a

big deal. The purpose of this call is to build a trusting relationship between you and him.

Step 6. See Them in Person

- Out of every 25 to 35 people you meet going door-to-door, only one or two will be open and receptive on these calls like our example of Ibrahim. That's normal.

- Make sure you see Ibrahim and any others open to you again. Return to their homes. Don't let them know you're coming, just show up. Don't have them make you dinner, but if they insist, it's polite to eat what is offered. Only you should eat, not everyone on the patrol. The locals have limited resources.

- After visiting Ibrahim, knock on the doors of several other houses on his street, so you don't draw attention to him. If you only visit Ibrahim's house then leave the area, neighbors will believe something is up, and Ibrahim's family may become a target for retaliation for helping the Americans. Be smart and creative in disguising those who are receptive to you.

Step 7. Repeat Daily

- Repeat the process above every day.

- Never be predictable in which streets or houses you'll knock on. Don't go to one street one day and the very next street the next day. Be random. Record the locations you target to make sure you haven't accidently fallen into a pattern. You don't want to end up in an ambush because you're being predictable. Record your sister platoon's targets for the same reason.

- You may speak with 15 to 25 people on one patrol, and then the same number on the phone the next day. Over the course of six months or so, you'll have a network of additional eyes and ears surrounding your combat outpost. They will fill you in on what's happening in the area.

BONUS! Go to **www.TacticalInfluenceBook.com** and download your free field guide which includes this checklist and script as a gift for reading this book.

Resources

Be a lifelong learner. Constantly strive to improve yourself through reading and thinking. Clearly, I am biased that you should read *this* book, but I want to provide you with some other must-read resources which have helped shape my thoughts and strategies, and which I believe will do the same for you. Below I've discussed what I enjoy about the top three resources, to help you understand what you're getting into. There are two books and one blog detailed, followed by some additional reading suggestions.

Influence: The Psychology of Persuasion by Robert B. Cialdini

This book is listed first for a reason: I re-read it every year. I first learned of Cialdini's book from a speech documented in the book *Poor Charlie's Almanac* (which is listed next), and immediately ordered it on Amazon. The original version published in 1984 was titled, *Influence: Science and Practice*, and the updated title appeared in later editions.

Cialdini writes in an easy-to-understand style about the various ways we all are influenced. He names six main factors at play in influence: reciprocity, commitment and consistency, social proof, liking, authority, and scarcity.

Everyone reacts to the different factors in varying degrees. For me, reciprocity is the biggest influencer. All my life, I've had this deep, burning desire to repay anyone who gives me something. Worse, I always felt I had to repay them quickly, and with more than I'd received. Before discovering Cialdini's book, I'd ask myself why I felt so compelled to repay people, and I never had an answer. I just knew I needed to, so I did—even when I really didn't want to. After reading the book, I understood. Even better, I knew *why* people use reciprocity to get what they want. Today, thanks to Cialdini's work, I am unaffected when a salesperson tries to use reciprocity on me.

Reciprocity isn't the only influencer, of course. Cialdini goes on to write about commitment and consistency, social proof, liking, authority, and scarcity. When I was attempting to counter an insurgency, I used them all! Let me give you some examples of how this worked.

Social proof: I'd tell people that their neighbors told me... (fill in the blank with some information my intelligence officer provided). I'd say everyone in the neighborhood is talking about it. Now, the person doesn't feel alone in telling me some nugget of information. They feel they are just like everyone else.

Liking: I wasn't mean. I didn't use fear tactics to get information from people. Depending on the needs and resources available, I offered them support, doctors, food, and supplies.

Scarcity: I'd tell them what would happen if al Qaeda took over. I'd talk about how their jobs would dry up and the electricity would be knocked out. I wouldn't threaten them with it; I'd just mention it in an honest, matter-of-fact way.

Commitment and consistency: By calling people every two weeks, I was consistent and committed to what I'd promised. I did what I said I'd do.

Authority: Okay, this is an easy one. I was the authority in their area.

If you read this book, you'll understand how other people use these elements of influence. You'll be better protected against them being used on you, and you'll be better prepared to use your influence when the situation requires it. These are so powerful, Cialdini has created "Principles of Ethical Influence." Check them out at www.InfluenceAtWork.com

Poor Charlie's Almanack: The Wit and Wisdom of Charles T. Munger edited by Peter D. Kaufman

This book contains a collection of speeches and talks Charlie Munger delivered throughout the second half of the 20th century. It's pretty cool stuff. This is not a book you casually open and read for a bit before falling asleep. No, this is a resource. It is wisdom, and it has some real heft to it—metaphorically and literally. It's almost too big to be a coffee table book, but if it is on your coffee table, you and I will have some great conversations!

As soon as you look for this book, you'll notice that it's pricey, but don't let that steer you away. It's worth the cost. You'll also see several versions available. As I write, the third edition is the most up-to-date, and that's the one I recommend. If Kaufman ever releases an update, I will buy it, whatever the price, and even if it only has one more speech or article. It really is that valuable.

Take your time going through this book. As you read, stop and think through Munger's words. Make notes. Ask yourself what you can learn from these speeches. And make sure you check out the best part: the resources section. Munger identified several books to read. Follow the rabbit hole of resources and you will be on your way to lifelong learning.

Farnam Street Blog

Farnam Street Blog, which you can find online at FS.blog, was started several years ago by Shane Parrish, who began the blog while working as a cybersecurity expert at Canada's top intelligence agency and pursuing a master's degree in business administration (MBA). He found the MBA program deficient in teaching what he expected, so he went out to pursue greater knowledge on his own. His pursuits led to reading about Charlie Munger and Munger's mental models approach to problem solving. Parrish started writing about what he was reading, and the Farnam Street blog was born. It became popular—really popular. Parrish hadn't disclosed his name back then. His site just listed a P.O. Box address, and people actually staked the box out to meet him. The blog has now grown to have a large following of very smart people, including CEOs and professional sports head coaches.

The website has a trove of free information on all things mental and rational. Its tagline is, "Helping you master the best of what other people have already figured out," and there are long and short articles that do just that. Parrish also has a free podcast in which he interviews really smart and accomplished people, asking them all kinds of challenging questions.

Checking the Farnam Street blog has become part of my weekly routine. It has helpful reading times listed for each article, so you know if you're getting into a long or short read. After reading the blog for several years, I had the pleasure of meeting Parrish one day, and he didn't disappoint. If there was one person I could have dinner with, it would be him.

Other Resources

I'd be honored if you reached out to me and shared your questions, thoughts, and results after reading this book. I'd love to be a resource for you. You can find me at **www.MitchellHockenbury.com** or on Facebook: **Tactical Influence the Book**.

The leaders of each military branch have their own reading lists, which you can look to for additional resources. I also recommend the following books:

- *Seeking Wisdom: From Darwin to Munger* by Peter Bevelin

This is a densely packed book and, as with *Poor Charlie's Almanack*, it is not for casual reading. Bevelin gives a synopsis of a topic and cites sources for additional reading, covering a range of really good stuff.

It's a fantastic book to use as a reference manual, and it helps me think through my decision-making process. I love to read a page, then stop and consider what I just learned. A pen and paper next to this book is a must. Take notes, and take your time going through it.

To broaden your perspectives:

- *Against the Gods: The Remarkable Story of Risk* by Peter L. Bernstein

- *Doughnut Economics: Seven Ways to Think Like a 21st-Century Economist* by Kate Raworth

- *Addiction by Design: Machine Gambling in Las Vegas* by Natasha Dow Schüll

- *The Silk Roads: A New History of the World* by Peter Frankopan

- *An Illustrated Book of Bad Arguments* by Ali Almossawi

My father. You taught me to care about others and to be humble.

My nieces and nephews. You make me proud watching you grow, and I am proud when you ask me to dispense advice. Thanks for listening (or pretending to).

The Josts:

Jason and Jenny. Thank you for showing me what evolved thought can bring. I swear I have come around to your way of thinking and it is not trivial that you were there first.

Sharon. Thank you for being on my side for all those years.

James. Your letters are an inspiration.

And Lastly

There are, of course, many folks I have not mentioned. I may not have listed you by name, but I am better off for having known and interacted with you. As I sit and reflect on the many people who have influenced me in life, I am humbled. I truly feel I am a reflection of some part of you.

Lastly, thank you for reading this book. It is my hope that there is one nugget you can take with you and use. I'm very grateful you chose to spend this time with me, and we are now connected, in a way. Thank you and God bless.

About the Author

Mitchell C. Hockenbury, MBA, CFP® is a career military man who was first enlisted in the Marine Corps and later commissioned in the Army as an Infantry Officer. He has multiple combat tours as an Infantry Platoon Leader during the surge of Iraq, and later, as an Infantry Company Commander where he led the last fighting force out of Iraq in December of 2011. He has been awarded numerous medals and badges. During his entire military career, he has worked with hundreds of soldiers to help improve their financial well-being.

Today, Mitchell is a fee-only financial planner with offices in Kansas City, MO and Omaha, NE, serving clients locally and across the country. Mitchell has a passion for helping others achieve their financial goals. He has the ability to translate complicated financial and investment strategies into plain English and works with individuals and families to create the plans to meet those goals.

You can find him at: **www.MitchellHockenbury.com**

Made in the USA
Middletown, DE
23 February 2023

25365973R00116